THE ENCYCLOPEDIA OF PSYCHOACTIVE DRUGS

IN 25 VOLUMES
Each title on a specific drug or drug-related problem

ALCOHOL
Teenage Drinking

THE ENCYCLOPEDIA OF PSYCHOACTIVE DRUGS

ALCOHOL

Teenage Drinking

ALAN R. LANG, Ph.D.

Florida State University

1985
CHELSEA HOUSE PUBLISHERS
NEW YORK

SENIOR EDITOR: William P. Hansen
ASSOCIATE EDITORS: John Haney, Richard Mandell
CAPTIONS EDITOR: Marian W. Taylor
EDITORIAL COORDINATOR: Karyn Gullen Browne
ART DIRECTOR: Susan Lusk
LAYOUT: Carol McDougall
ART ASSISTANTS: Ghila Krajzman, Tenaz Mehta
PICTURE RESEARCH: Juliette Dickstein
COVER PHOTO: Frank Lusk

First Printing

Library of Congress Cataloging in Publication Data
Lang, Alan R.
    Alcohol, teenage drinking.
    (The Encyclopedia of psychoactive drugs)
    Bibliography: p.
    Includes index.
    1. Youth—Alcohol use—United States.   I. Title.
II. Series.
HV5135.L36   1985   363.2′922′088055   85–7826

ISBN 0-87754-761-0

Chelsea House Publishers
Harold Steinberg, Chairman & Publisher
Susan Lusk, Vice President
A Division of Chelsea House Educational Communications, Inc.

Chelsea House Publishers
133 Christopher Street
New York, NY 10014

Photos courtesy of Alcoholics Anonymous World Services, Inc. (pp. 107 and 115
© 1977; reprinted with permission), AP/Wide World Photos, The Bettmann
Archive, National Institute on Alcohol Abuse and Alcoholism, Joseph E. Seagram
and Sons, Inc., UPI/Bettmann Newsphotos, and *USA Today* (p.48 © 1984, p.100
© 1985; reprinted with permission).

CONTENTS

A Salt Lake City cocktail waitress sports a T-shirt bearing a clear message. Wherever liquor is sold in Utah, state law requires the posting of a warning about the potential hazards of alcohol consumption.

8

FOREWORD

In the Mainstream of American Life

The rapid growth of drug use and abuse is one of the most dramatic changes in the fabric of American society in the last 20 years. The United States has the highest level of psychoactive drug use of any industrialized society. It is 10 to 30 times greater than it was 20 years ago.

According to a recent Gallup poll, young people consider drugs the leading problem that they face. One of the legacies of the social upheaval of the 1960s is that psychoactive drugs have become part of the mainstream of American life. Schools, homes, and communities cannot be "drug proofed." There is a demand for drugs—and the supply is plentiful. Social norms have changed and drugs are not only available—they are everywhere.

Almost all drug use begins in the preteen and teenage years. These years are few in the total life cycle, but critical in the maturation process. During these years adolescents face the difficult tasks of discovering their identity, clarifying their sexual roles, asserting their independence, learning to cope with authority, and searching for goals that will give their lives meaning. During this intense period of growth, conflict is inevitable and the temptation to use drugs is great. Drugs are readily available, adolescents are curious and vulnerable, there is peer pressure to experiment, and there is the temptation to escape from conflicts.

No matter what their age or socioeconomic status, no group is immune to the allure and effects of psychoactive drugs. The U.S. Surgeon General's report, "Healthy People," indicates that 30% of all deaths in the United States

Tennessee law calls for a 48-hour jail sentence for all first-offense drunk drivers. In addition, offenders such as this man must spend time "sleeping it off" in the county sheriff's "drunk tank."

are premature because of alcohol and tobacco use. However, the most shocking development in this report is that
mortality in the age group between 15 and 24 has increased
since 1960 despite the fact that death rates for all other age
groups have declined in the 20th century. Accidents, sui-
cides, and homicides are the leading cause of death in young
people 15 to 24 years of age. In many cases the deaths are
directly related to drug use.

THE ENCYCLOPEDIA OF PSYCHOACTIVE DRUGS an-
swers the questions that young people are likely to ask
about drugs, as well as those they might not think to ask,
but should. Topics include: what it means to be intoxicated; how drugs affect mood; why people take drugs; who
takes them; when they take them; and how much they
take. They will learn what happens to a drug when it enters
the body. They will learn what it means to get "hooked"
and how it happens. They will learn how drugs affect their
driving, their schoolwork, and those around them—their
peers, their family, their friends, and their employers. They
will learn what the signs are that indicate that a friend or a
family member may have a drug problem and to identify
four stages leading from drug use to drug abuse. Myths
about drugs are dispelled.

National surveys indicate that students are eager for
information about drugs and that they respond to it. Students not only need information about drugs—they want
information. How they get it often proves crucial. Providing young people with accurate knowledge about drugs is
one of the most critical aspects.

THE ENCYCLOPEDIA OF PSYCHOACTIVE DRUGS syn-
thesizes the wealth of new information in this field and
demystifies this complex and important subject. Each volume in the series is written by an expert in the field.
Handsomely illustrated, this multi-volume series is geared
for teenage readers. Young people will read these books,
share them, talk about them, and make more informed
decisions because of them.

Miriam Cohen, Ph.D.
Contributing Editor

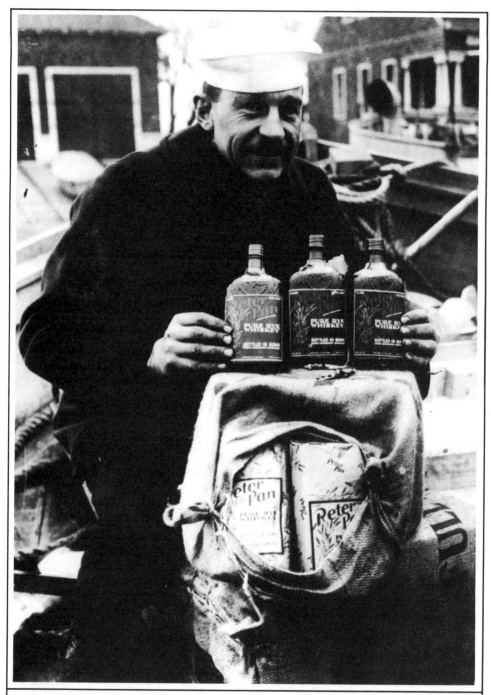

Following an all-night battle in 1930, a Coast Guardsman displays a sample of the 3,000 cases of liquor seized from a heavily armed Lake Erie rum-runner during a Prohibition liquor bust.

INTRODUCTION

The Gift of Wizardry
Use and Abuse

JACK H. MENDELSON, M.D.
NANCY K. MELLO, PH.D.
Alcohol and Drug Abuse Research Center
Harvard Medical School—McLean Hospital

Dorothy to the Wizard:

"I think you are a very bad man," said Dorothy.
"Oh, no, my dear; I'm really a very good man; but I'm a very bad Wizard."
—from THE WIZARD OF OZ

Man is endowed with the gift of wizardry, a talent for discovery and invention. The discovery and invention of substances that change the way we feel and behave are among man's special accomplishments, and like so many other products of our wizardry, these substances have the capacity to harm as well as to help. The substance itself is neutral, an intricate molecular structure. Yet, "too much" can be sickening, even deadly. It is man who decides how each substance is used, and it is man's beliefs and perceptions that give this neutral substance the attributes to heal or destroy.

Consider alcohol—available to all and yet regarded with intense ambivalence from biblical times to the present day. The use of alcoholic beverages dates back to our earliest ancestors. Alcohol use and misuse became associated with the worship of gods and demons. One of the most powerful Greek gods was Dionysus, lord of the Underworld and god of wine. The Romans adopted Dionysus but changed his name to Bacchus. Festivals and holidays associated with Bacchus celebrated the harvest and the origins of life. Time has blurred the images of the Bacchanalian festival, but the theme of drunkenness as a major part of celebration has survived the pagan gods and remains a familiar part of modern society. The term "Bacchanalian festival" conveys a more appealing image than "drunken orgy" or "pot

13

party," but whatever the label, some of the celebrants will inevitably start up the "high" escalator to the next plateau. Once there, the de-escalation is difficult for many.

According to reliable estimates, one out of every ten Americans develops a serious alcohol-related problem sometime in his or her lifetime. In addition, automobile accidents caused by drunken drivers claim the lives of tens of thousands every year. Many of the victims are gifted young people, just starting out in adult life. Hospital emergency rooms abound with patients seeking help for alcohol-related injuries.

Who is to blame? Can we blame the many manufacturers who produce such an amazing variety of alcoholic beverages? Should we blame the educators who fail to explain the perils of intoxication, or so exaggerate the dangers of drinking that no one could possibly believe them? Are friends to blame—those peers who urge others to "drink more and faster," or the macho types who stress the importance of being able to "hold your liquor"? Casting blame, however, is hardly constructive, and pointing the finger is a fruitless way to deal with problems. Alcoholism and drug abuse have few culprits but many victims. Accountability begins with each of us, every time we choose to use or to misuse an intoxicating substance.

It is ironic that some of man's earliest medicines, derived from natural plant products, are used today to poison and to intoxicate. Relief from pain and suffering is one of society's many continuing goals. Over 3,000 years ago, the Therapeutic Papyrus of Thebes, one of our earliest written records, gave instructions for the use of opium in the treatment of pain. Opium, in the form of its major derivative, morphine, remains one of the most powerful drugs we have for pain relief. But opium, morphine, and similar compounds, such as heroin, have also been used by many to induce changes in mood and feeling. Another example of man's misuse of a natural substance is the coca leaf, which for centuries was used by the Indians of Peru to reduce fatigue and hunger. Its modern derivative, cocaine, has important medical use as a local anesthetic. Unfortunately, its increasing abuse in the 1980s has reached epidemic proportions.

The purpose of this series is to provide information about the nature and behavioral effects of alcohol and drugs, and the probable consequences of both their moderate use and abuse. The authors believe that up-to-date, objective information about alcohol and drugs will help readers make better decisions as to whether to use them or not. The information presented here (and in other books in this series) is based on many clinical and laboratory studies and observations by people from diverse walks of life.

Over the centuries, novelists, poets, and dramatists have provided us with many insights into the beneficial and problematic aspects of alcohol and drug use. Physicians, lawyers, biologists, psychologists, and social scientists have contributed to a better understanding of the causes and consequences of using these substances. The authors in this series have attempted to gather and condense all the latest information about drug use and abuse. They have also described the sometimes wide gaps in our knowledge and have suggested some new ways to answer many difficult questions.

One such question, for example, is how do alcohol and drug problems get started? And what is the best way to treat them when they do? Not too many years ago, alcoholics and drug abusers were regarded as evil, immoral, or both. It is now recognized that these persons suffer from very complicated diseases involving deep psychological and social problems. To understand how the disease begins and progresses, it is necessary to understand the nature of the substance, the behavior of the afflicted person, and the characteristics of the society or culture in which he lives.

The diagram below shows the interaction of these three factors. The arrows indicate that the substance not only affects the user personally, but the society as well. Society influences attitudes towards the substance, which in turn affect its availability. The substance's impact upon the society may support or discourage the use and abuse of that substance.

SUBSTANCE
(ALCOHOL OR DRUG)

PERSON ◄─────────► SOCIETY

Although many of the social environments we live in are very similar, some of the most subtle differences can strongly influence our thinking and behavior. Where we live, go to school and work, whom we discuss things with—all influence our opinions about drug use and misuse. Yet we also share certain commonly accepted beliefs that outweigh any differences in our attitudes. The authors in this series have tried to identify and discuss the central, most crucial issues concerning drug use and misuse.

Regrettably, man's wizardry in developing new substances in medical therapeutics has not always been paralleled by intelligent usage. Although we do know a great deal about the effects of alcohol and drugs, we have yet to learn how to impart that knowledge, especially to young adults.

Does it matter? What harm does it do to smoke a little pot or have a few beers? What is it like to be intoxicated? How long does it last? Will it make me feel really fine? Will it make me sick? What are the risks? These are but a few of the questions answered in this series, which, hopefully, will enable the reader to make wise decisions concerning the crucial issue of drugs.

Information sensibly acted upon can go a long way towards helping everyone develop his or her best self. As one keen and sensitive observer, Dr. Lewis Thomas, has said,

"There is nothing at all absurd about the human condition. We matter. It seems to me a good guess, hazarded by a good many people who have thought about it, that we may be engaged in the formation of something like a mind for the life of this planet. If this is so, we are still at the most primitive stage, still fumbling with language and thinking, but infinitely capacitated for the future. Looked at this way, it is remarkable that we've come as far as we have in so short a period, really no time at all as geologists measure time. We are the newest, the youngest, and the brightest thing around."

AUTHOR'S PREFACE

Most books and articles on teenage drinking are not written for young people. Instead, they are aimed at parents, teachers, counselors, and others who frequently deal with youth and their problems. This failure to address directly the teenagers themselves incorrectly suggests that, at least where alcohol use and its problems are concerned, young people cannot or should not be held responsible for their own actions. Promoting such an idea does a great disservice to the vast majority of teenagers who, when provided with the facts with which to make informed choices, and treated with respect, are capable of acting in a responsible manner.

Until society begins to dispel the association between drinking and lack of responsibility, it will continue to suffer destructive consequences. For example, while there may be some benefit from raising the legal drinking age, this effort to "protect" young people by reducing their access to alcohol does little to help teenagers develop the kinds of attitudes and habits that might result in the prevention of alcohol problems. Moreover, the unsuccessful enforcement of drinking age laws is liable to produce less responsible citizens, for both teenagers and adults come to view the rules of society with disrespect and contempt.

While these points about teenage drinking seem obvious, one may wonder why adult society persists in its ill-advised attitudes about alcohol and the prevention of its misuse. One goal of this book is to shed some light on this issue by considering everything from history, economics, and politics, to some of the key principles of social psychology. Despite the wide scope of these subjects, one conclusion emerges: *This society is ambivalent about alcohol.* It cannot decide whether or not to treat it as a drug. It is unclear about who should use it, what and where it is appropriate, how much is too much, what defines a drinking problem, and how a drinking problem should be treated. People cannot even agree on how or why drinking affects the way a person feels or acts. With regard to alcohol use, the only thing about which American society seems certain is alcohol's ambiguous status. No wonder it is difficult to make decisions about drinking!

This book is not intended to justify American drinking behaviors, attitudes, or beliefs. Rather, it should provide a better understanding of the current facts and viewpoints about alcohol, and stimulate thoughts about how we might use this new insight to decrease and/or eliminate our drinking problems.

Another goal of this book is to explain and clarify the effects commonly associated with drinking. This includes an analysis of people's common beliefs and expectations, as well as a description of the physiological and psychological mechanisms involved in producing alcohol's effects. In addition, the patterns of alcohol use and abuse in the United States will be discussed, including a summary of how these patterns are affected by such factors as age, gender, family background, peer relations, and personality. Finally, some alternative strategies for the prevention of alcohol abuse will be presented, together with the evidence necessary to evaluate their effectiveness.

All the information will focus on or be related to teenagers, with the hope that it will provide the knowledge and understanding that will encourage informed decisions about drinking alcohol.

A national park visitor investigates a Prohibition-era still in Maryland's Catoctin Mountains. Such equipment produced millions of gallons of "moonshine," or illegal whiskey, during the 1920s.

America's attitudes toward alcohol consumption have varied over the years, but obvious abusers, as depicted in this drawing, have generally been regarded with scorn. Only in recent years have medical groups such as the AMA come to consider alcoholism as a treatable disease.

CHAPTER 1

ALCOHOL AND ITS HISTORY IN AMERICA

*T*he critical ingredient common to all alcoholic beverages is ethyl alcohol or ethanol. It is a clear, almost tasteless liquid formed through the fermentation of sugars by yeast spores. The amount of alcohol produced depends on the type and amount of sugar in the original mixture, the type of yeast used, and the temperature maintained during the fermentation process. American beers, which contain about 3% to 6% alcohol, are made from malted barley and hops (the ripened and dried cones of the hop plant). Most wines are made by fermenting grapes or berries, and normally reach a maximum of about 15% alcohol, though they are sometimes "fortified" with additional ethanol alcohol and thus may reach 20% alcohol in sherry or port wines.

Other more potent beverages, such as whiskey, often have grains (e.g., corn) as a basic ingredient, but must use a distillation process to increase their alcohol content. To do this the fermenting mixture, or "mash," is heated in a closed container so that the ethanol—which has a low boiling point—can be vaporized, separated, and then reliquified by cooling. While it is possible to produce pure ethyl alcohol by this process, most distilled spirits actually contain about 40% to 50% alcohol. The exact percentage of ethanol in any hard liquor can be determined by dividing the proof, as listed on the bottle's label, by two. Thus, for example, 80 proof liquor is 40% ethanol.

The History of Alcohol in America

Though alcoholic beverages and their effects have been known to the world for thousands of years, significant drinking in the United States is a far newer phenomenon. It was probably the European traders, settlers, and colonists who first introduced widespread alcohol use to America. Despite this brief history, however, drinking patterns and popular beliefs about the nature of alcohol's effects and the causes of alcohol-related problems have undergone dramatic changes. A brief review of these changes might help to explain some of the ambivalence and uncertainty that plague current attitudes about drinking.

During the approximately 150 years between the colonial period and the Revolutionary War, alcohol was generally regarded as a "Good Creature of God." It was used as a medicine and praised for its contribution to a sense of warmth, relaxation, and good fellowship. Local inns and taverns served as seats of community government and as meeting places for entire families, isolated from one another in the largely agricultural society of the day. Drinking was

Amidst a scene of drunkenness and debauchery, two innocent ragged and barefoot children wait in a saloon while their pitchers are refilled with beer. Such images were widely used by anti-saloon activists during the 19th century.

part of the social fabric of colonial America.

This is not to say there were no problems associated with drinking. Indeed, frequent heavy drinking, drunkenness, and idleness were commonplace. The prevailing attitude, however, was one of acceptance—people needed breaks from the demands of everyday life, and alcohol was readily available, so drinking was tolerated or even encouraged. During this time no one saw alcohol as the cause of any social problems. In fact, only a few religious leaders objected to drinking, and even they confined their criticisms to habitual drunkards, whom they regarded as lacking in moral fiber. They claimed that the fault was not in the alcohol, but rather was in the moral weakness of the person who needed only motivation and discipline to reform him or herself. Accordingly, the problem drinkers of the colonial period were preached at or publicly humiliated and punished to help them see "the error of their ways."

As post-Revolutionary War America began to mature, it grew more populated and industrialized. In this period of expansion drinking habits and attitudes also changed. Inns and taverns, formerly the meeting places of middle-class

Smirking evilly, "Demon Rum" himself surfaces to tempt the weak with a glass of his wicked brew. The association of the Devil with alcohol predates to ancient times.

families and the socially elite, greatly increased in number and assumed a new image. Saloons became lower- and working-class gathering places, dominated by men who now labored in factories or as hired help, rather than on a family farm. Separated all day from wives and children, these men also spent their leisure time away from home and family. Bars became centers for prostitution and gambling, places where middle- and upper-class men went only to "slum."

This new character of the tavern was intensified by the growing structure of an industrialized society. Workers could no longer set their own schedules and integrate small amounts of drinking into their days as they pleased. Thus, the times

The "drunkard's cloak" was one of the more fanciful devices created in the 19th century to keep tipplers sober. Temperance workers sometimes advanced rather extreme ideas. For example, some insisted that if exposed to a match, the blood of a drinker would instantly burst into flames.

and places for drinking became limited, and so each opportunity to drink was more liable to result in a heavy drinking binge. Taken together, the changing atmosphere of the tavern and the reduced opportunities for alcohol consumption led to a pattern of drinking that associated alcohol with a lack of respectability and self-control. Otherwise decent people seemed to be transformed by drink into irresponsible savages, prone to crime, violence, and general immorality.

By the mid-1800s temperance groups had begun to flourish. They were led by religious figures discontented with the lack of self-control which liquor had come to symbolize, and by women whose families were threatened by the new tavern and all that it represented. This powerful temperance movement promoted a view of drinking that was remarkably different from that of the "Good Creature of God" period. It was the "Demon Rum" era, when not the man, but the alcohol itself was to blame for problems associated with drinking. It was assumed that alcohol was an

A New York City delegation in Washington, D.C., demonstrates against proposed Prohibition legislation in 1919. Urban males were among the most outspoken opponents of the 18th Amendment.

addicting poison for *anyone* who drank it. Even the most moderate and controlled persons placed themselves at risk whenever they touched a drink to their lips. The supporters of temperance, who saw alcohol and its sale as a public menace and believed a nation of abstainers would be our only salvation, gradually applied their political muscle. Finally, when the 18th Amendment and the Volstead Act became law in 1920, national prohibition became a fact of American life after World War I. Alcohol was no longer legal.

However, federal prohibition was considered a failure largely due to inadequate enforcement and the resulting profitability of black market liquor production and distribu-

A prospective customer is eyed by the cautious doorkeeper of a 1930s speakeasy, or illegal bar. While Prohibition did succeed in reducing the nation's alcohol consumption, it also created many new problems for social and law enforcement agencies. For example, before the 18th Amendment was ratified, Washington, D.C., had 300 licensed bars; afterward it had 700 speakeasies.

tion by organized criminal elements. By 1933 it was re-
pealed and a new perspective on alcohol and drinking
emerged—the so called "disease concept of alcoholism,"
which represents something of a compromise between the
"Good Creature" and the "Demon Rum" views. It holds that
for the vast majority of people alcohol is indeed the relatively harmless substance used in colonial America. However, the disease concept also maintains that there is an
unfortunate minority for whom alcohol acts as the addicting
poison opposed by the prohibitionists. This unique vulnerability to alcoholism is allegedly based on genetic or biologic
defects rather than on some more general moral weakness
in the affected individuals.

Today the disguises worn by New York City Prohibition detectives "Izzy"
Einstein (at left) and "Moe" Smith seem preposterous. However, in the 1920s
these "thieves" successfully mingled with bootleggers and thus gained fame
for their undercover work in the battle against alcohol.

Thus, the appropriate response to drinking problems is neither punishment for the drunkard nor prohibition of alcohol for those who can safely handle it. It is instead the provision of medical help to those who supposedly have no control over their drinking. Though other views of alcohol misuse—particularly those which consider abuse a more general public health problem—have gained some momentum in recent years, the disease concept of alcoholism is still the most prevalent one in the United States today.

There are three key points to stress in this historical review. Firstly, it reveals that America's ambivalence about alcohol has a historical basis. America has been through periods when alcohol and its effects were seen as generally good for society, as totally bad for society, and as good for some members of society but bad for others. Secondly, the changes in attitudes from one period to the next depended on the social, economic, and political climate—*not* on an important scientific discovery that significantly altered our objective knowledge or understanding about alcohol and its associated problems. Thirdly, it is important to recognize that each of these historical perspectives still influences our attitudes and policies about drinking. Compulsory treatment and/or punishment of public drunkards continue to reflect a moralistic intolerance of relatively harmless deviant behavior. Extensive and complicated laws and regulations that seek to control alcohol production and distribution suggest a bit of the temperance mentality as well, though radical prohibition is seldom advocated.

Meanwhile, a strange partnership of alcohol manufacturers and alcohol treatment providers has formed to promote the popular, but unsubstantiated, view that all drinking problems are due to alcoholism. Oddly, this restricted view of alcohol problems, in which the problems are associated with a chronic and irreversible disease to which only a small minority of the population is susceptible, has benefits for both groups. It allows the alcoholic beverage industry to promote its profitable product to the supposedly invulnerable majority of people. And at the same time, those who provide treatment, and thus have a vested interest in the disease concept of alcoholism, are provided with an economically and politically powerful ally in their efforts to focus attention and resources on alcoholism treatment, rather than on alternative approaches to the problems of drinking.

Clearly, the varied history of American drinking patterns and problems, including ever-changing attitudes and policies that have developed in connection with them, offers a foundation on which to build a better understanding of alcohol use in the United States today. And teenage drinking is no less affected by this history than anyone else's.

Beer drinkers toast the end of Prohibition, which was cheered in most U.S. cities. Writer H.L. Mencken called the 18th Amendment "the work of ignorant bumpkins of the cow states who resented the fact they had to swill raw corn liquor while city slickers got good wine and whiskey."

In 1949 a bar patron contributes to the National Committee for Education on Alcoholism, one of the first groups to consider alcoholism a disease instead of a moral weakness. Many organizations, including the American Medical Association, regard alcoholism as a disease.

CHAPTER 2

EXPECTATIONS ABOUT ALCOHOL AND ITS EFFECTS

American history and its associated government policies offer no clear and uniform message about drinking. This ambiguity is further complicated by the many informal, and often inconsistent, norms or sets of rules that have developed amid the uncertainty. These may depend on such factors as the age, gender, race, ethnic background, religion, and social class of the group with which one identifies at any particular time. Given the great size and diversity of the American society, it should not be too surprising that drinking expectations and habits vary widely between groups. Indeed, research shows that young people drink more than older people, men drink more than women, and more whites drink than blacks. The drinking patterns of French-Americans are vastly different from those of Turkish-Americans, a higher proportion of Catholics than Jews are alcoholics, and rich people drink different types of alcoholic beverages than the poor.

Despite the fact that knowledge of such group identifications may make expectations about drinking more certain, it is often unwise to make assumptions. People can change due to events that are active (e.g., getting married), passive (e.g., getting older), or incidental (e.g., getting richer or poorer). Regardless of their changeability, however, these long-term group associations may not be as critical to drinking expectations as the highly variable, short-term influences of the immediate social situations and physical surroundings in which one finds oneself. For instance, a young man's friends may expect and perhaps even pressure him to drink very heavily on the night before his wedding, while the same classmates or business associates probably would think it inappropriate to do any drinking before a major examination or job interview.

Research evidence also shows that drinking rates are related to less obvious social factors, such as the size of the group and the ratio of males to females in the group. Similarly, studies of the relation between the physical surroundings and drinking in bars suggest that more alcohol is consumed where there is live rather than taped or jukebox music, when lighting is moderate rather than low or bright, and when the decor is action-oriented rather than filled with the more inactive portraits or landscapes. The price of a drink is also likely to have a strong effect on expectations about drinking.

The discussion of drinking expectations should serve to illustrate some of the many factors that make decisions about drinking so confusing. Rather than being a simple all-or-none choice, what one typically is deciding is under which circumstances drinking is appropriate, and also how much drinking might be acceptable, desirable, or "normal." Personal and group characteristics as well as social and

These four St. Louis drinkers made local news when they claimed—and proved—that each of them regularly consumed five cases of beer a week. Researchers report that teenagers who abuse alcohol do most of their drinking with companions away from home, and that they drink less when adults are present.

physical dimensions of the immediate situation often play a role in these decisions. However, the potential drinker may not be readily aware of their influence.

Important as these objective features of ourselves and the environment might be, decisions about drinking also depend in large measure on your subjective beliefs or expectations about what will happen if you do drink. Naturally, who you are and what you have been told, have observed, or have directly experienced in relation to drinking will help shape these expectations. So will your perception of cues present in the environment. To the extent that you believe drinking will have mainly positive effects, including anything from a quenching of thirst to a greater sense of social comfort, you will be disposed to drink. On the other hand, if you expect more negative effects, from a bad taste in the mouth to an embarrassing display to vomiting, you will be inclined not to drink.

Interestingly, the range of expectations people have about the effects of drinking is almost as diverse and variable as the drinkers themselves and the drinking situations in which they find themselves. Some expectations are for good effects and some are for bad effects, but many may be regarded as either good or bad depending on who has them and under what circumstances. Further examination of these expectations about alcohol's effects should provide a better understanding of the attractiveness of drinking.

Expectations about the Effects of Drinking

It seems safe to say that one of the expected effects of consuming at least a moderate amount of alcohol is that it will produce an "altered state of consciousness." In other words, one can expect to feel different after drinking. This is one of the defining properties of all psychoactive drugs, and perhaps the most important one. Some theorists have even argued that this ability to change one's psychological state is the only explanation needed to understand why alcohol and other drugs are used. They assert that, by nature, human beings seek and enjoy the experience of altered states of consciousness. The frightening or unpleasant elements are ignored or forgotten, and this seductive sense of "differentness" persists. Even as children many enjoy spinning to the point of dizziness or riding roller coasters which rearrange one's insides, despite the fact that, or perhaps because, these activities often scared us. Thus, getting anxious or depressed, speeded up or slowed down, highly sensitized or greatly dulled, may all be a welcome relief from an "intolerably boring state of sameness."

While this general hypothesis about the natural reinforcement of altered states of consciousness is not without merit, it does not seem to be a sufficient explanation for alcohol use. Most people's lives have at least some variety, and much drinking takes place with other people. So it may be necessary to consider some more specific social expectations to get a complete picture of what factors influence the decision to drink.

In recent years alcohol research has increasingly focused on the nature and development of expectations about the effects—especially the anticipated positive effects—of drinking. The objective has been to examine not only the relation between an individual's expectations of alcohol's effects and his or her patterns, usual drinking, but also to explore how these expectations might influence the feelings and behaviors that *actually* accompany and follow drinking. While this connection with actual effects will be reviewed later, what follows is an examination of the expectations themselves.

Beginning in the late 1970s, several teams of investigators began surveying various groups of subjects to determine what expected effects of alcohol were most common. One study focused on the positive or reinforcing expectations in adults, and identified six major categories of beliefs:

- alcohol generally alters experiences in a positive way
- alcohol adds to social or physical pleasure
- alcohol contributes to sexual experiences and performances
- alcohol increases aggression and dominance
- alcohol improves sociability and social assertiveness
- alcohol reduces tension

The first two factors are rather broad in nature and are most closely associated with persons who described themselves as light drinkers. Heavier and more frequent drinkers, on the other hand, placed greater emphasis on the more specific expected effects mentioned in the final four categories, perhaps indicating they learned to expect these reactions through extensive direct drinking experiences.

Several other studies, surveying adults ranging from college students to older alcoholics, have identified various behavioral impairments (e.g., clumsiness, delayed responsiveness, and decreased memory or concentration) among the expected negative effects of drinking—especially heavy drinking. The positive expectations were quite similar to those in the six categories listed above. Though many of the adolescents had had little or no drinking experience, their expected effects and those of adult drinkers were remarkably consistent.

The expected effects of alcohol, reported by three age groups of young people, are summarized in Table 1. Clearly, most of the expectations were present *before* there had

Many drinkers expect alcohol to improve their sociability. In fact, it may be the expectation itself that gives alcohol this property.

Table 1

Expected Effects of Alcohol

12- TO 14-YEAR OLDS
Reduces tension
Impairs motor (physical) functioning
Changes social and emotional behavior (both positively and negatively)
Increases aggression and sense of power
Distracts attention from worries
Arouses emotion and causes loss-of-control in interpersonal behavior
Generally alters experiences in a positive way
Adds to physical and social pleasure

15- TO 16-YEAR-OLDS
Adds to physical and social pleasure
Changes social and emotional behavior (both positively and negatively)
Generally alters experiences in a positive way
Increases aggression and sense of power
Impairs motor (physical) functioning
Reduces tension
Distracts attention from worries
Increases assertiveness and carefree interpersonal behavior

17- TO 19-YEAR-OLDS
Contributes to sexual experiences and performances
Increases aggression and sense of power
Reduces tension
Distracts attention from worries
Changes general experiences (both positively and negatively)
Changes social and emotional behavior (both positively and negatively)
Adds to physical and social pleasure

SOURCE: Adapted from Christiansen, et al.,
Journal of Consulting and Clinical Psychology, vol. 50, pp. 336–44. ,1982

been much direct experience with alcohol. Age and greater drinking experience seemed only to focus expectations developed through observations of drinkers and through information obtained from families, peers, and the media.

Research has also discovered that young people with drinking problems seem to hold a fairly strong belief that alcohol improves their intellectual and physical performance. Nondrinkers or nonproblem drinkers from the same age group did not share this expectation, though they did believe alcohol could improve their social functioning.

It is interesting that many of the expectations—such as that alcohol will make you more sociable and more likely to pick a fight, more sleepy and a better lover, or more coordinated and more clumsy—appear to be contradictory. These contradictions should lead one to question whether or not the alcohol itself *directly* causes all, some, or even any of the expected effects. This is an especially relevant question to raise as one focuses beyond the physical or bodily effects and begins to look at the influence of drinking on social interactions.

Where behavior towards and feelings for other people are concerned, it seems likely that more than just the alcohol is involved. This is supported by the fact that people have systematically different expectations about alcohol's effects, depending on what type of beverage (beer, wine, mixed drinks or straight drinks) they are asked to consider. This is the case even though ethanol is the active ingredient in all of the drinks and, though different quantities may be required (depending on the alcoholic content), the same level of intoxication can be reached with any alcoholic drink. People tend to associate more pleasant events (e.g., romance or celebrations) with wine, while they think of negative outcomes (e.g., illness or drowning one's sorrows) in connection with straight drinks of distilled spirits.

All these expectations and situational factors contribute to what might be called the "social meaning" of drinking, which, as we have already seen, is quite complicated and ambiguous for the American drinker.

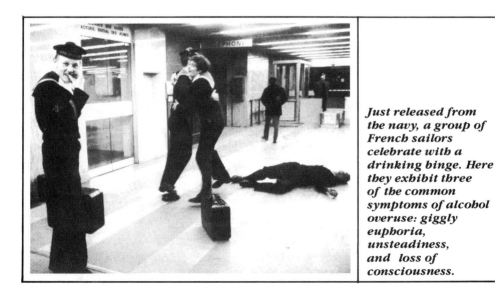

Just released from the navy, a group of French sailors celebrate with a drinking binge. Here they exhibit three of the common symptoms of alcohol overuse: giggly euphoria, unsteadiness, and loss of consciousness.

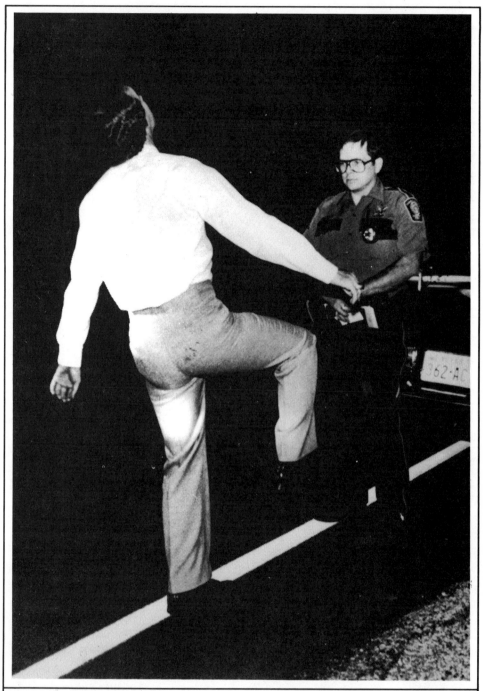

A police officer watches a suspected drunk driver take a sobriety test. Such tests usually require subjects to walk a straight line. Imbalance and lack of coordination are key signs of alcohol intoxication.

CHAPTER 3

THE SHORT-TERM EFFECTS OF ALCOHOL

While expectations can help shape one's reaction to drinking, it is clear that alcohol has its own direct effects. It is a powerful drug, capable of affecting body and behavior. The determining factor is how much ethanol is in the bloodstream, because it is via the blood that alcohol is carried to the brain, nervous system, and bodily organs and systems where its direct action takes place. It is believed that one critical effect of alcohol is to increase the rigidity of the members of neurons (nerve cells), making it difficult for impulses to pass. This partially explains why a person feels and acts differently when drunk.

The amount of alcohol in the blood, which determines an individual's level of intoxication, is typically referred to as the blood-alcohol concentration (BAC) or the blood-alcohol level (BAL). Both terms mean the same thing and refer to the proportional weight (in milligrams, or 1/1000 of a gram, abbreviated mg) of alcohol per 100 volumes (in milliliters, abbreviated ml) of blood. BAC is usually expressed as a percentage, so that 100 mg of alcohol per 100 ml of blood would be written as 100 mg%. However, popular references to BAC, including legal definitions of "intoxication," ordinarily change the milligrams to grams (e.g., 100 mg becomes .10 g) and then leave the grams out. Thus, 100 mg% becomes a blood-alcohol concentration of 0.10%. This simplified method of expression is the one that will be used here.

What Determines BAC?

Obviously, before people can have a concentration of alcohol in their bloodstreams they first must ingest some alcohol. For most this is accomplished by drinking alcoholic beverages. The ethanol is absorbed within the digestive tract, especially by the stomach (20%) and the small intestine (75%). Only about 5% is excreted in the urine.

The rate at which alcohol enters the blood is influenced by any factor that affects the absorption process. For instance, consuming very diluted alcoholic beverages and/or drinking on a full stomach tends to slow down absorption, since it takes longer for the ethanol to reach the intestine. And the carbonation in beverages, by relaxing the stomach valve which allows material to move into the intestine, speeds up the rate of absorption. Though nearly all alcohol consumed will eventually be absorbed, rates are important because rapid absorption produces higher peak (though briefer) BACs; while slow absorption rates result in longer-lasting, but lower peak BACs.

Once in the bloodstream, ethanol is rapidly and uniformly distributed within all body fluids, including those in the fetus of a pregnant woman. Almost immediately, the body, perceiving the alcohol as a foreign substance, begins acting to eliminate it from the bloodstream. The liver is the main organ involved in this process. As elimination progresses, enzymes (catalysts present in the body) metabolize, or break down, alcohol, first into highly toxic and volatile acetaldehyde, and then into acetate, which can be converted either to energy or to various usable body substances.

The rate of metabolism remains fairly constant for an individual regardless of activity level. However, it can be influenced by one's general health and physical condition, as well as by any history of heavy drinking. In general, the average person takes up to two hours to metabolize or eliminate about two-thirds of an ounce, or the amount of ethanol in a standard-sized beer, glass of wine, or single shot of hard liquor.

Given this basic understanding of how the body responds to alcohol, it is now possible to discuss the major factors that contribute to BAC. Three important factors are what, how much, and how fast one drinks.

Alcoholic beverages differ in the concentration of ethanol they contain: beers average 4.5%, wines about 12%, and straight distilled spirits (hard liquor) approximately 40%. As previously noted, very diluted alcoholic beverages are absorbed more slowly than concentrated ones. And in addition, if you drink equal volumes of the three types of alcoholic beverage, you consume quite different amounts of ethanol.

These facts often lead people to believe they will get less drunk on beer than on wine, and less drunk on wine than on hard liquor. However, this conclusion is made without recognizing that the actual volume of alcohol included in an average drink is also different. A typical beer is 12 ounces; the usual glass of wine contains 4 or 5 ounces; and the average hard-liquor drink has a single shot (1½ ounces) of distilled spirits. Calculating from the total volume of these standard-sized drinks and the average concentration of alcohol in each type, it is readily seen that there are almost equal amounts of ethanol, or approximately .6 ounces, in one beer, one glass of wine, and one single straight or mixed drink of hard liquor. Therefore, because they all contain roughly the same amount of alcohol, they are all capable of producing very similar BACs. In short, the type of alcoholic beverage being drunk is not nearly as critical to BAC as the number of drinks consumed.

If you drink a lot of beer, you drink a lot...

Manufacturers of wine and beer—but not of distilled spirits—may advertise their products on television, a fact that leads some people to assume that beer and wine consumption is not really "drinking."

The speed with which the alcohol is drunk is also important. For example, a higher peak BAC will occur by having three drinks in one hour than by spreading them over several hours. Because alcohol is rapidly absorbed, drinking quickly and in rapid succession results in a sudden, high BAC. Whereas, because the body is constantly metabolizing the alcohol, slower or spaced drinking gives the body a chance to "burn up" the alcohol already in the system before more is introduced. Thus, the amount of time spent drinking, as well as the total amount of alcohol consumed, is also critical to BAC.

The final major factors that influence BAC are the drinker's body weight and, to a lesser extent, the proportion of the body weight that is fatty tissue. These are critical because ethanol is distributed evenly into all body fluids, including the blood. Therefore, since a large part of human body weight is fluid, the heavier person will have more fluid within which to distribute whatever alcohol is consumed. The result is that if both a 100-pound and a 200-pound person were to drink equal amounts of ethanol, the lighter individual would attain a BAC that is almost twice that of the heavier person. This is why larger people do not seem to get as intoxicated as smaller ones who drink the same amount.

Thus, if males tend to be able to "hold their liquor" better than females, the difference is partly due to the fact that the average male is heavier than the average female.

A smiling couple takes part in the pastime sometimes called "happy hour." Studies indicate that in the 1950s American drinking patterns began to shift. Once associated mainly with parties and bars, cocktail consumption was becoming a common activity at home.

Table 2

Effect of Body Weight and Rate and Volume of Alcohol Consumption on BAC (in %)						
AFTER ONE HOUR OF DRINKING						
NO. OF DRINKS	BODY WEIGHT (lbs.)					
	100	120	140	160	180	200
1	.03	.03	.02	.02	.02	.01
2	.06	.05	.04	.04	.03	.03
3	.10	.08	.07	.06	.05	.05
4	.13	.10	.09	.08	.07	.06
5	.16	.13	.11	.10	.09	.08
6	.19	.16	.13	.12	.11	.10
AFTER THREE HOURS OF DRINKING						
NO. OF DRINKS	BODY WEIGHT (lbs.)					
	100	120	140	160	180	200
2	.02	.01	.01	.00	.00	.00
3	.06	.04	.03	.02	.01	.01
4	.10	.07	.06	.04	.03	.03
5	.13	.10	.08	.06	.05	.04
6	.17	.13	.11	.09	.07	.06
7	.20	.16	.13	.11	.09	.08
8	.24	.19	.16	.13	.11	.09
9	.27	.22	.18	.15	.13	.11
10	.30	.25	.21	.17	.15	.13
11	.34	.28	.23	.20	.17	.15
12	.37	.31	.26	.22	.19	.17

NOTE: One drink is equal to one 12 oz. beer, one 5 oz. glass of wine, or one 1½ oz. shot of 80 proof liquor.

Also contributing to this difference is the fact that a greater proportion of male body weight is made up of fluids, whereas females, by nature, generally have more low-fluid fat and less high-fluid muscle. For this reason even a female weighing exactly the same as a male might reach a higher BAC than the male who has more fluid in which to dissolve the same amount of alcohol. The differences due to tissue content, however, are relatively small.

Table 2, which uses the average weights of males and females, illustrates how amount of alcohol consumed, rate of consumption, and body weight operate together to determine BAC.

Intoxication

Much has been written about the acute (short-term) effects of alcohol on the body and on physical and mental performance. Bodily reactions such as vomiting and behaviors such as staggering and slurred speech are most commonly associated with drunkenness. These and other similar effects and their relationship to specific levels of BAC are summarized in Table 3.

These effects mainly reflect the action of alcohol as a general depressant of the central nervous system, which includes the brain and spinal cord. Alcohol reduces the ability of neurons (nerves) to produce and transmit electrical impulses essential for the proper processing of information that comes to the brain from the skin, senses, and muscles; information relayed within the brain and necessary for thinking; and information that the brain sends to different parts of the body to control all bodily functions.

Teenagers toast the sponsor of a 1973 Illinois law reducing the wine- and beer-drinking age to 19. However, some studies suggest that the number of drinking problems decrease when the minimum age is higher.

Table 3

Effects of BAC on the Body and Performance	
BAC (%)	EFFECT
.01–.05	Increase in neural excitability and heart/respiration rates Decrease in various brain center functions Inconsistent effects on behavioral task performances Decrease in judgment and inhibitions Mild sense of elation, relaxation, and pleasure
.06–.10	Physiological sedation on nearly all systems Decreased attention and alertness, slower reactions, impaired coordination, and reduced muscle strength Reduced ability to make rational decisions or exercise good judgment Increase in anxiety and depression Decrease in patience
.10–.15	Dramatic increase in reaction time Impairment of balance and movement Slurred speech Vomiting, especially if this BAC is reached rapidly
.16–.29	Severe sensory impairment, including reduced awareness of external stimulation Severe motor impairment, e.g., frequent staggering or falling
.30–.39	Nonresponsive stupor Loss of consciousness Anesthesia comparable to that for surgery Death (for some)
.40 & up	Unconsciousness Cessation of breathing Death, usually due to respiratory failure

NOTE: The relation between BAC and its effect may vary considerably, depending on how rapidly the BAC was reached, whether BAC is increasing or decreasing, and the person's drinking history.

There is some evidence to suggest that at low BACs some stimulating, as opposed to depressing, effects of intoxication may be experienced. There is considerable controversy about why this occurs, but the existence of a two-phased action of alcohol—initial stimulation followed by depression—could help explain why people have contradictory expectations about alcohol's effects. It may be that at certain low BACs people are aroused, excited, and stimulated, while subsequent, higher BACs cause them to become sedated, anesthetized, and depressed. Thus, people may be attracted to drinking mainly because of the initial stimulation period, but become depressed because they do not know when to stop.

A few of alcohol's short-term effects on the body's systems other than the central nervous system require special attention. Many people believe that a cocktail before dinner will improve one's dining pleasure and, in fact, there may be some truth to this claim. A small amount of alcohol does stimulate the production of gastric (stomach) juices and thus may increase appetite. However, anything beyond a single drink has the reverse effect. Even moderate levels of intoxication involve enough alcohol to irritate the stomach lining and reduce the action of digestive organs, thereby hindering digestion. In addition, this same amount of alcohol also deadens one's sense of taste. And of course, rapid drinking of large quantities of alcohol may stimulate the vomit reflex, and this self-protective reaction ordinarily does not add to one's dining pleasure.

In connection with digestion, it is worth mentioning that pure alcohol contains a great many calories (about 200 per ounce). However, alcoholic beverages typically contain few vitamins or minerals and have little nutritional value. Therefore, they are not readily stored for rebuilding the body, but they can be used for energy production. This is an important fact, because it means that the foods you eat while drinking alcoholic beverages are more likely to be stored in body tissue, while the body uses alcohol's calories

A float in an anti-prohibition parade features a biblical quotation recommending the use of wine. Both "wets" and "drys" used the scriptures to back up their arguments.

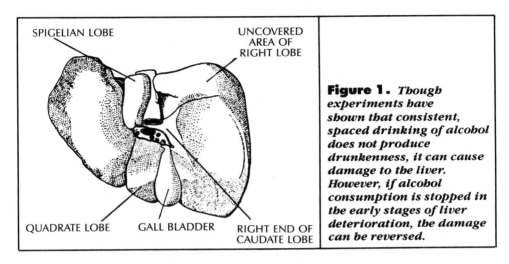

SPIGELIAN LOBE   UNCOVERED AREA OF RIGHT LOBE

QUADRATE LOBE   GALL BLADDER   RIGHT END OF CAUDATE LOBE

Figure 1. *Though experiments have shown that consistent, spaced drinking of alcohol does not produce drunkenness, it can cause damage to the liver. However, if alcohol consumption is stopped in the early stages of liver deterioration, the damage can be reversed.*

for energy. Obviously, this can lead to weight problems and is one of the main reasons most diets specifically exclude alcoholic beverages. Therefore, "beer bellies" are not so much a direct effect of the beer one drinks, but of food that is eaten with the beer.

The heart and circulation are also affected by acute doses of alcohol. As noted previously, at low BACs there may be a slight increase in heart rate and also blood pressure. At higher levels, a decrease occurs, and irregularities in heart function, especially its rhythm, are fairly common. Alcohol dilates (enlarges) blood vessels at the body's surface. This is sometimes noticeable as a reddening of the skin and an increased sense of warmth. However, drinking actually increases heat loss and thus reduces the core body temperature, leaving muscles and internal organs with less blood. Therefore, drinking alcohol to keep warm can be dangerous—while feeling warm you could freeze to death.

In addition to the depressing effect of alcohol on the central nervous system, alcohol-related reactions of the endocrine (gland) system may also be involved. In the presence of alcohol the pancreas secretes an excess of the hormone insulin, and as a result sugars in the blood may be broken down too rapidly. At the same time, alcohol reduces production of glucose (a type of sugar) by the liver. Together these effects can cause hypoglycemia (low blood sugar), characterized by low energy, increased anxiety, and other psychological effects.

Increased urination, another common effect of drinking, is also influenced by hormones released from glands. Though fluid intake during drinking does in itself increase the need for urination, in the presence of alcohol the pituitary gland releases a hormone that reduces the amount of fluid retained by the kidneys. Hence, one urinates more. This hormone effect, however, occurs only while BAC is rising.

Another pituitary hormone, oxytocin, which helps control milk secretion and uterine contractions in women, is affected by alcohol. In this case, drinking alcohol inhibits release of the hormone, which results in a reduction of mammary gland flow (which impedes breast feeding) and uterine contractions (which affects normal delivery). Other aspects of reproductive and sexual functioning affected by alcohol will be considered in Chapter 4.

As should be clear from the association of sensory impairment, depression, sedation, stuttering, etc., with intoxication, alcohol influences one's mental and physical performance of practical tasks. As indicated in Table 3, at BACs above .15% significant effects of alcohol on all aspects of functioning occur. In fact, such high levels of intoxication

To increase public awareness of the dangers posed by drunken drivers, both private and governmental agencies use cartoons, pamphlets, billboards, and other advertisements. The National Commission Against Drunk Driving reported that half of the nation's 43,918 motor vehicle fatalities in 1984 were alcohol-related.

are associated with a "reversible brain syndrome" in which learning and memory, abstract reasoning, and perceptual organization are all greatly (though temporarily) impaired. A major reduction in voluntary control of physical motion and reaction also occurs at this high BAC level, and the intoxicated person may even be immobilized.

What is perhaps more important—and dangerous—are the effects of intoxication that accompany BACs low enough to give the person the false confidence to participate actively in practical tasks. Of course, all activities—such as swimming, bicycling, and operating power tools or other dangerous machinery—have some potential for accidents, but driving an automobile while under the influence of alcohol is especially dangerous because many lives are often at risk.

An anti-drunk driving billboard paid for by the State of Pennsylvania next to a liqueur advertisement clearly illustrates the conflicting messages that people use as a basis for their drinking-related decisions.

Experimental studies of the effects of drinking on driving have suffered from the fact that it is difficult to simulate actual driving conditions either in the laboratory or on a closed driving course. One problem is that to some extent subjects can compensate for alcohol-induced impairments if they are motivated to do so, as in an experimental situation. It is fair to assume, however, that while driving on the road such motivation and concentration would tend to fade, and so impairment would increase. This assumption is supported by the fact that one of the effects of intoxication is the reduction of the ability to maintain continuous attention. Therefore, the decreases in driving performance observed in experimental studies probably *underestimate* those that actually occur under more natural driving circumstances.

One of the most consistent findings of alcohol and driving research is that on *divided attention tasks* impairment of functioning is dose-related—as BAC increases, performance decreases. Divided attention tasks are those that require subjects to do several things at once, such as maintaining constant speed while responding to signals that demand a specific turn or other reaction, depending on the nature of the signal. These divided attention tasks can be thought of as a complex combination of several simple tasks.

At BAC of .10% it may be fairly easy to do one or two well-practiced, simple maneuvers, such as driving along a road and turning at predictable points. The risks of drinking and driving, however, are magnified when the unexpected occurs: a car suddenly turns in front of you, someone runs a red light, or oncoming traffic shifts into your lane. Then you must divide your attention between simple steering, recognizing the new situations, making decisions about what to do, and carrying out the proper actions. It is in these more complex and demanding circumstances that higher BACs predict increased impairment of driving ability and risk of accidents.

Alcohol also makes the driver's performance more erratic. Intoxicated drivers are more variable in their behavior, making frequent adjustments in speed, direction, following distance, and so on. They have difficulty staying "on task." Thus, while their average performance may seem acceptable, the many minor deviations or errors they make and then correct (or overcorrect) increase their vulnerability to

The nation's crackdown on drunken driving took an unusual twist with the arrest of Will Hammet, a 69-year-old working cowboy. Hammet was charged with riding a horse while intoxicated in Stockton, California.

accidents. This same pattern is typical of many new drivers who have not yet mastered the skill of operating a car and so tend to be insecure and thus make many errors. Therefore, drinking by inexperienced or otherwise poor drivers is particularly risky.

There are several other direct effects of alcohol on driving-related skills. Because at higher BACs reaction time is slowed, the driver's ability to discriminate or distinguish between levels of light or sound and to estimate the speed and distance of moving objects is impaired, and general body coordination is reduced. During night driving drinkers also have more difficulty with glare since their eyes are slow to adapt to changes in light. Obviously, any of these changes increase the likelihood of having an accident.

The last, and perhaps more problematic, connection between drinking and driving is that the intoxicated person typically fails to recognize the alcohol-induced impairment.

FRIENDS DON'T LET FRIENDS DRIVE DRUNK

STOP DWI

A California ambulance attendant questions the injured driver of a sports car crushed by an out-of-control pickup truck. The truck's driver, also hurt in the wreck, was booked for drunken driving.

Driving is not avoided, and once behind the wheel the intoxicated driver feels excessively confident of his or her abilities, taking more risks than when sober. There can be little question that these errors in judgment, coupled with alcohol-induced impairment of the capacity to process essential information and to control the vehicle, account for a significant number of auto accidents.

Sobering Up and the Hangover

Once a high BAC has been reached and no additional alcohol is consumed the sobering up process can take place. Actually, as noted earlier, the metabolism of alcohol begins as soon as alcohol enters the bloodstream and is circulated through the liver. Sobering up is just a continuation of this process. The same factors that influence BAC and absorption of alcohol also help determine how long it will take to become sober. Obviously, the more one drinks the longer it will take for all the alcohol to be cleared out of the system. Though drinking on a full stomach results in a lower BAC than if the same amount of alcohol was ingested on an empty stomach, the slower absorption does mean that there will be alcohol in the system for a longer time, since it cannot be metabolized until it gets into the blood. The question that logically follows is, how can the sobering up process be speeded up?

Unfortunately, there is almost nothing you can do to get sober more quickly, other than vomiting any alcohol still in the stomach before it gets absorbed. Drinking coffee or tea might make you *feel* more awake, but in reality you will be just as drunk and impaired for just as long. The same can be said of exercising or taking a cold shower. The only thing (other than maybe a blood transfusion) which truly helps is the passage of time. At best, the body can metabolize no more than about one-third ounce of ethanol in an hour, so it may take two hours to eliminate the alcohol from each standard-sized drink. The body will continue working at this rate until all the alcohol is gone. Then all you have to worry about is the hangover.

Though most people who have ever had a drink of alcohol have, to some extent, experienced a hangover, remarkably little is known about what causes it. The symptoms of headache, fatigue, upset stomach, thirst, anxiety, depression, and irritability are quite variable, but all are unpleasant. Some experts believe that an excess of fluid in the brain causes the headache, that low blood sugar results in fatigue, and that the insults to the digestive system might account for the upset stomach. Disruption of fluid balance in the body as a whole and within individual body cells could contribute to thirst. And, of course, someone with all these physical symptoms would generally feel unwell and so might get unpleasant psychological effects. Other theories blame hangovers on a build-up of toxic acetaldehyde after drinking, or on the chemical impurities in alcoholic beverages. No one knows for sure what is responsible, but the

We who make and sell whiskey say "TONIGHT WHEN IT'S ONE FOR THE ROAD BE SURE IT'S COFFEE"

THE HOUSE OF SEAGRAM
FINE WHISKIES SINCE 1857

Preoccupied with their public image, the liquor industry's public-relations department has responded to the rising concern about highway deaths attributable to alcohol. One result is a distiller-sponsored advertising campaign urging consumers to use alcoholic beverages in moderation.

problem gets worse as the age of the drinker increases.

The cure of hangovers is, unfortunately, about the same as for sobering up—there is not much you can do but wait. Taking another drink ("the hair of the dog that bit you" method) only postpones the hangover. Vitamins, coffee, raw foods, and other home remedies do not work either. Only time, and maybe aspirin along with rest and a bland diet, will lead to eventual recovery from hangovers.

Mixing Alcohol and Other Drugs

Any review of the acute effects of drinking would not be complete without some mention of possible interactions of alcohol with other drugs. Because many people do not think of alcohol as a drug that produces the powerful physiological effects discussed above, they do not realize that if in addition to alcohol they ingest anything from over-the-counter drugs to prescription medication to illicit substances, they are actually mixing two or more drugs. Depending on the specific drug in question, alcohol may oppose, add to, or multiply the effects of the other drug.

Some prescription drugs, for example, are made useless because alcohol counteracts their effects. When alcohol and another drug share some effects, those effects may be twice as intense when the two are taken together. This is the case, for instance, with the sedative action of alcohol and antihistamines. Most dangerous, however, are the synergistic, or super-additive, interactions of alcohol with some other drugs. In this case when the two drugs are taken together there is more than a simple additive effect. In fact, the effects may be multiplied many times. One example is the combination of alcohol and barbiturates or other sedatives (e.g., sleeping pills or other "downers"). Even at a BAC as low as .10% this combination could so depress the central nervous system that death could result. Such potentially fatal interactions can occur with antianxiety and sleeping medications of the benzodiazepine class, such as Valium or Dalmane. The reasons for this dramatic kind of unexpected effect are not altogether clear, but the message should be—never guess at the possible interactions of alcohol and other drugs. The consequences could be fatal.

Moderate use of alcohol may not be dangerous to one's health, but addiction to this drug can cause irreparable damage. Today more than 9 million Americans suffer from alcoholism.

CHAPTER 4

THE LONG-TERM EFFECTS OF ALCOHOL

*I*n addition to the acute effects of intoxication on the body and on performance, important physiological and behavioral changes may occur with chronic (long-term) alcohol use, especially if heavy drinking is involved. Many of these consequences are the result of years of drinking at a high level, but some are not. Since most teenagers are relatively new consumers of alcohol, focus will be on those effects of repeated drinking that develop rather quickly. It should be emphasized that one need not be an alcoholic to experience changes due to chronic alcohol consumption.

Tolerance

One result of recurring drinking episodes over a prolonged period of time is the development of *tolerance*. Tolerance has developed if the drinker requires more alcohol to experience the same effects he or she used to get, or if when the drinker consumes the same amount of alcohol as he or she used to, not as much effect is experienced. More simply, the alcohol-tolerant person can "hold," "handle," or "not show" his or her liquor.

One explanation for this effect is that the body, especially the liver, adapts to the frequent introduction of alcohol and is able to metabolize it more rapidly. Thus, what is called *metabolic tolerance* is developed. While this may contribute to tolerance, it would suggest that tolerant drinkers do not reach or maintain as high a BAC as nontolerant people, and this is why they can drink more. However, there is considerable evidence that experienced drinkers also show *behavioral tolerance*, that is, their behavioral performances are not as impaired as those of inexperienced drinkers even when both groups have the same BAC. Apparently, one can learn how to compensate for some of the effects of alcohol as experience with acting while under the influence increases.

There are, of course, limits to behavioral tolerance, but there can be little doubt that it contributes to individual differences in the effects of drinking. This fact should be kept in mind when considering the effects of various BACs listed in Table 3. These only represent *average* reactions, and the occasional drinker may be as impaired at .05% as the moderate drinker is at .07% or as the heavy drinker at .10%. The drinker must learn his or her own limits.

One final kind of alcohol tolerance is *cross-tolerance.* In this case alcohol's actions cause a reduced responsiveness to other drugs. Though the mechanisms of this effect are not well understood, some research has shown that when long-

A Japanese man seems oblivious to a pair of drinkers who lie unconscious in front of vending machines that dispense sake, wine, and whiskey in the Sanya district. This ghetto, not far from Ginza, a famous shopping district in Tokyo, is an island of poverty and despair.

term heavy drinkers are sober, they are more difficult to anesthetize and generally do not show as great a reaction to barbiturates, benzodiazepine, sedatives, and other similar drugs.

In addition to tolerance acquired through drinking experience, a person's tolerance to alcohol may be affected by physical condition, fatigue, or the stress that he or she is under while drinking. As noted earlier, various aspects of the social situation and physical surroundings can also play a role. But in addition, people are simply born with differences that determine responses to alcohol. For instance, research has shown that Asian people show more negative responses to acute intoxication than do Caucasians. On the other hand, recent studies suggest that children of alcoholics may find alcohol to be more effective in reducing their responses to stress than do children of nonalcoholics. Tolerance to alcohol can vary even among children in the same family, as does tolerance to pain.

Dependence and Withdrawal

Alcohol is a potentially addictive drug, and prolonged abuse of it may result in a physical dependence. This dependence may not be apparent until the drinker stops or dramatically cuts down consumption, after which a characteristic set of reactions known as a *withdrawal syndrome* occurs. Within 8 to 12 hours after drinking ceases, and for as long as 3 to 5 days, symptoms may include tremors ("shakes"), sweating, nausea, vomiting, sleep disturbances, and general irritability. Much less common are seizures (convulsions or "fits") and delirium tremens or DTs (characterized by confusion, disorientation, hallucinations, and intense physiological arousal), which do not begin until 2 or 3 days after drinking stops. If untreated, the DTs are fatal in as many as 20% of the cases.

Proper alcohol detoxification ("drying out"), or the process of clearing the body of the alcohol and its associated effects, typically includes a medical examination followed by the necessary treatment, good nutrition, rest, and vitamin supplements. It may also involve the administration of drugs that produce effects similar to alcohol. Because of their cross-tolerance to alcohol, these drugs slow down withdrawal and thus reduce the severity of the withdrawal symptoms, making it easier on the body and the patient.

Additional Problems
Associated with Chronic Drinking

Given the extent of the acute effects of alcohol on body systems and organs, it should not be too surprising that repeated drinking can have very serious physical consequences. Chronic drinking can kill brain cells, change brain structure, and reduce the supply of blood to the brain. Alcohol also robs the body of thiamine (a B vitamin) and other vitamins critical to brain functioning. As a partial consequence the chronic drinker may experience premature aging.

Alcohol's central nervous system damage also includes problems with coordination, movement, and perception, confused and disorganized thinking, and significant loss of memory functioning. This type of memory problem is different from a blackout, or failure of the sober individual to recall events that happened during a period when he or she was

Passed out on a street in Gallup, New Mexico, this unidentified man represents an increasingly severe problem in many U.S. cities: a shortage of jail cells to house people arrested for public drunkenness.

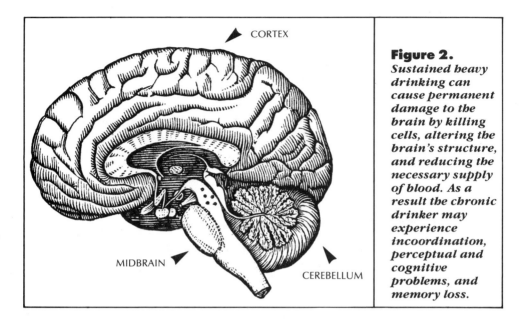

CORTEX

MIDBRAIN

CEREBELLUM

Figure 2.
Sustained heavy drinking can cause permanent damage to the brain by killing cells, altering the brain's structure, and reducing the necessary supply of blood. As a result the chronic drinker may experience incoordination, perceptual and cognitive problems, and memory loss.

intoxicated. Blackouts are probably not due to permanent brain damage, though most experts do agree they are associated with excessive drinking.

Because the liver is so central to the body's processing of alcohol, it is an organ greatly affected by chronic drinking. Fat deposits, caused by the effect of alcohol on the body's handling of fats, may accumulate in the liver and interfere with its functioning. Hepatitis (liver inflammation) can also result from prolonged heavy drinking, producing pain and liver damage that sometimes can be fatal. Cirrhosis of the liver is the disease most commonly associated with alcoholism. It involves the development of scar tissue to replace those parts of the liver damaged by excessive inflammation and other disease-related symptoms. It is *not* reversible and greatly decreases essential functions of the liver, such as clearing the body of toxic substances, increasing the risk of early death.

Chronic drinking can also damage the digestive system, which, due to the resultant difficulty in processing nonalcoholic foods, may lead to malnutrition. In addition, heavy drinkers often substitute many "empty" alcohol calories for nutritious foods which could be stored and used to rebuild the body. Excessive alcohol use has also been linked to many heart, gland, and muscle diseases, as well as to a significantly increased risk of cancer. It seems to be especially destructive if the drinker also smokes cigarettes.

The life expectancy and the quality of life of chronic heavy drinkers is markedly reduced. However, some data indicate that moderate drinkers (those who consume two or fewer drinks per day) actually may have a lower risk of heart attack and certain other circulatory problems than abstainers. It seems that for an adult a drink or two a day probably will not cause any direct harm. Of course, this assumes that the alcohol drinker avoids driving or being involved in other potentially dangerous situations.

Birth Defects and Fetal Alcohol Syndrome

As mentioned previously, when alcohol is absorbed it is distributed to all body fluids, including those of a pregnant woman's fetus and the placenta which nourishes it. Because of this, the developing unborn child is introduced to alcohol and to all of the physiological consequences of alcohol intoxication that the mother may experience. However, for at least two reasons the effects on the fetus may be even greater than those on the mother. Firstly, the fetus does not have the same level of tolerance as the mother. Secondly, the impact of alcohol on the sensitive growth and development process of the infant is much greater than that on an adult drinker.

Research on the offspring of women who are heavy drinkers has now documented the significantly increased risk of birth defects and developmental problems in these children. The specific set of defects resulting from alcohol consumption during pregnancy has been termed Fetal Alcohol Syndrome (FAS) and may include (1) central nervous system problems, including mental retardation, undersized head and brain, poor physical coordination, irritability, and overactive behavior; (2) growth deficiencies in both height and weight, before and after birth; (3) facial abnormalities such as short eye slits, droopy eyelids, thin upper lip, and mid-face and jaw deformities; and (4) poorly formed organ systems, including heart, kidney, genital, bone, and joint.

Alcohol-abusing women are more likely than others to have miscarriages, premature deliveries, and stillbirths (babies born dead).

While Fetal Alcohol Syndrome and the pregnancy and birth difficulties of drinking women are serious, what is more frightening is the likelihood that alcohol-related birth defects are not restricted to heavy-drinking mothers. There is now evidence that pregnant women who drink as little as a drink or two a day may have more miscarriages and deliver smaller babies who grow more slowly and have more behavioral difficulties than those of abstinent mothers. Thus, it appears that *any* drinking by a pregnant woman may increase the risk of birth defects, and heavier drinking only exacerbates the problem.

These facts argue that any woman who is even actively *attempting* to become pregnant should consider abstaining from alcohol. If she waits until she confirms her pregnancy before stopping, she may have already exposed her baby to the damaging effects of alcohol.

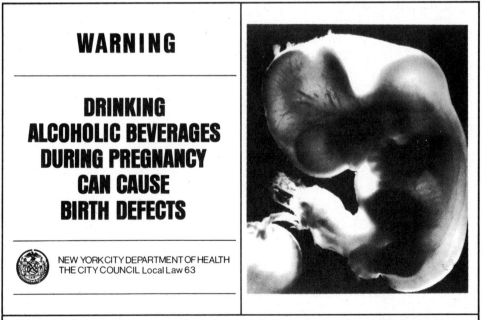

WARNING

DRINKING ALCOHOLIC BEVERAGES DURING PREGNANCY CAN CAUSE BIRTH DEFECTS

NEW YORK CITY DEPARTMENT OF HEALTH
THE CITY COUNCIL Local Law 63

This 45-day-old human embryo is especially vulnerable to agents such as alcohol that can cause birth defects. Because of this many communities require that signs like this one be displayed wherever liquor is sold.

Bill Spangler, a hard-drinking, 66-year-old West Virginian who describes himself as a man in "pitiful shape," fits the stereotype of the alcoholic. In fact, most alcoholics are not derelicts or "skid row" residents. Recent studies indicate that 70% of America's alcohol addicts live what would otherwise be seen as "respectable" lives.

CHAPTER 5

SOCIAL PSYCHOLOGY AND DRINKING BEHAVIOR

*E*ven a casual reading of the preceding section describing alcohol's direct effects on the body and on physical and mental performance should make one wonder why anyone would drink to excess. Who wants to lose the ability to perceive the environment, to make complicated decisions, or to react quickly and in a coordinated manner? Who enjoys risking accidents? Who likes to vomit or suffer from a hangover? Who wants to suffer brain damage, liver disease, or even death?

One would hope that the answer is no one, and yet all these can be direct consequences of drinking, which so many of us do. Moreover, the earlier discussion of both adults' and teenagers' expectations of alcohol's effects indicated that at least some behavioral impairments and other negative consequences are anticipated by most drinkers. But careful examination of those expectations (see Table 1) reveals something else. Most of the expectations, and probably the major motivations for drinking, have to do with the association between the effects of alcohol and social behavior. The following sections will review existing theory and research on the relation between drinking and sociability, sexuality, and aggression, the most important social behaviors influenced by alcohol consumption. In addition, mention will also be made of how drinking affects mood.

Basic Principles

In order to analyze drinking and social behavior it is important to understand the kinds of factors that might influence their relationship. This is facilitated by using a general model that experts on alcohol and other drugs frequently use. It is called the *agent-host-environment model.* Simply stated, it assumes that the level of any drug's use and also its effects are determined by a combination of the specific effects of the agent (in this case, alcohol), the characteristics of the host (the user or drinker), and the nature of the environment (including the effect of social and physical features on drinking).

The direct effects of the agent alcohol have already been detailed, as have some characteristics of the host drinker (e.g., tolerance) that influence reactions to alcohol. However, it will be necessary to discuss how environmental factors might help determine the amounts people drink. Thus, the model will make use of familiar information, with a new emphasis on how these kinds of factors interact in social situations.

A key principle of psychology that is important here is that *any behavior is affected by its consequences.* In other words, if a behavior is associated with pleasure or is in some way rewarded, it will tend to increase. If, on the other hand, a behavior has unpleasant associations or is punished, it will tend to decrease. These facts are no less true of drinking. As shall be seen, this principle helps to explain not only why people drink, but also why they sometimes act the way they do when drinking.

Overview of Drinking and Social Effects

There is little doubt that the circumstances in which one drinks can influence the kinds of reactions one experiences. Perhaps the simplest demonstration of this fact was an experiment investigating the effects of alcohol on mood. All participants drank the same type and amount of alcoholic beverage, either while alone or while with a group. They were then asked to describe how they felt during the period of intoxication. The differences were striking. Those who drank alone stressed the changes in their physical/mental states (dizziness and unclear thinking), but when drinking took place in a social situation the participants reported changes in mood and interpersonal behavior (e.g., less unhappy and more friendly). Thus, while the physiological reactions to alcohol were not different under the two conditions, i.e., all participants reached approximately the same BAC, the social and psychological responses were clearly influenced by environmental cues picked up by the drinker.

Since in our culture alcohol consumption is associated with a wide variety of social situations, the available environmental cues are quite different depending on when and where one drinks. And, in turn, the social and psychological reactions to drinking in the presence of those cues could be quite different as well. For example, at a party the cues might encourage sociability. But drinking with a girl- or boyfriend in a quiet, romantic place, may stimulate sexual feelings. A hot, loud room crowded with guys from a rival

Net-stockinged waitresses take orders in the Gaslight Club, a New York City nightspot whose 19th-century decor is intended to inspire uninhibited and relaxed behavior. Research findings show that the atmosphere in which alcohol is consumed has a strong influence on its perceived effects.

gang or football team might elicit aggressiveness in drinkers.

Therefore, many behaviors previously assumed to be directly related to drinking or intoxication are probably only *indirect* effects of alcohol. That is, the effects cannot be totally explained in terms of the direct or specific action of the drug. This conclusion helps explain the apparently contradictory expectations one can have regarding alcohol's effects—they *all* may be true, depending on the situation. It also enables us to understand why we do not always have the same reactions to drinking—the environmental cues are not always the same.

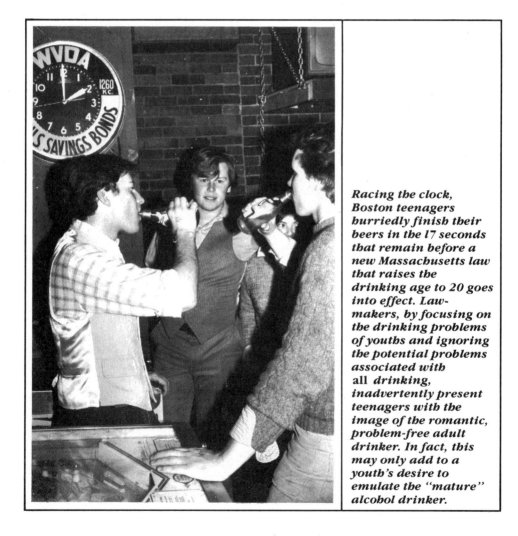

Racing the clock, Boston teenagers hurriedly finish their beers in the 17 seconds that remain before a new Massachusetts law that raises the drinking age to 20 goes into effect. Lawmakers, by focusing on the drinking problems of youths and ignoring the potential problems associated with all *drinking, inadvertently present teenagers with the image of the romantic, problem-free adult drinker. In fact, this may only add to a youth's desire to emulate the "mature" alcohol drinker.*

Through our own actual drinking experiences and through extensive exposure to models of drinking, observed directly as well as in advertisements, television, movies, and other media, we have many opportunities to learn certain associations between drinking and social behavior. Especially in the media, the message is that drinking is the key to being popular, sexually attractive, independent, strong, or courageous—characteristics most of us would like to have. Thus, people are encouraged to drink, and alcohol may acquire such strong "social meaning" through these associations to these characteristics that it can become a cue for sociability, sexuality, and aggression, regardless of the fact that its biological action may have little to do with these behaviors. Even in the absence of alcohol the presence of drinking cues may be sufficient to produce changes in one's behavior.

Research Methods

How can the direct physiological effects of alcohol (or any drug) be separated from those that are due to the psychological expectations and environmental cues? One sophisticated way of approaching this problem is through the use of a "balanced placebo" study. In this type of study the participants are led to believe that the drinks they are consuming are either alcoholic or nonalcoholic, while in fact they may or may not be alcoholic. The experimenter then records the reactions of each participant, noting which type of beverage was consumed and its role in the study—active, placebo, anti-placebo, or control (see Figure 3). In such experiments vodka and tonic are usually chosen because it is easy to hide the taste of vodka if it is mixed with enough cold tonic.

A comparison of the drinkers' reactions across the four possible combinations of expected beverages and actual beverages received permits the experimenter to determine how much of the effect was caused by the direct action of alcohol and how much was due to the person's expectations. What follows are some balanced-placebo studies of how drinking affects three of our most important social behaviors.

Sociability and Social Anxiety

Most Americans believe people often become more sociable when drinking. Alcohol is available and its consumption encouraged by hosts and sponsors at so many kinds of gatherings or events where people are expected to interact that it has come to be regarded as a "social lubricant." Increased social pleasure, assertiveness, talkativeness, and even happiness are all expected by many when they drink in these situations. The most popular explanation for these effects is that alcohol reduces tension or anxiety, probably by depressing the nervous system and thereby reducing inhibitions. This, in turn, allows the drinker to feel more relaxed and comfortable in social situations, which also encourages the drinker to drink more when under stress.

As reasonable as this may sound, studying the direct effect of alcohol on physical tension (e.g., muscle tension) and on anxiety (e.g., increased heart rate) often has not supported this explanation. It has even been shown that in certain circumstances drinking can *increase* tension and anxiety. This suggests that environmental cues and psychological factors such as expectation may play a role in the association between drinking and degree of sociability. Several balanced-placebo experiments test this hypothesis.

In the first experiment researchers selected a group of male college students who were social drinkers. Each was given a few drinks of either tonic only or a mixture of vodka and tonic, along with instructions which led them to expect that they were drinking either alcoholic or nonalcoholic drinks. In some cases the expectation was accurate, while in others it was not. After drinking his beverages, each man was introduced to a young woman and was asked to do his best to make a good impression on her. And during each interaction the pair was observed and the man's heart rate was measured. This provided an opportunity to test social anxiety. After the conversation was over, each man was asked to describe the feelings he had while talking to the woman.

The results showed that in comparison to men who expected only tonic water (anti-placebo or control), those who *thought* they had received vodka in their drinks— regardless of whether they actually had or not (active or

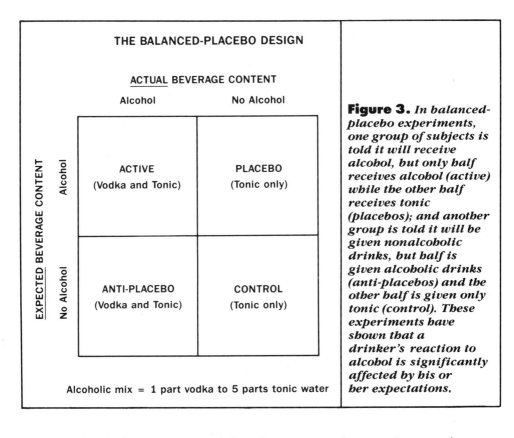

THE BALANCED-PLACEBO DESIGN

ACTUAL BEVERAGE CONTENT

	Alcohol	No Alcohol
Alcohol	ACTIVE (Vodka and Tonic)	PLACEBO (Tonic only)
No Alcohol	ANTI-PLACEBO (Vodka and Tonic)	CONTROL (Tonic only)

EXPECTED BEVERAGE CONTENT

Alcoholic mix = 1 part vodka to 5 parts tonic water

Figure 3. *In balanced-placebo experiments, one group of subjects is told it will receive alcohol, but only half receives alcohol (active) while the other half receives tonic (placebos); and another group is told it will be given nonalcoholic drinks, but half is given alcoholic drinks (anti-placebos) and the other half is given only tonic (control). These experiments have shown that a drinker's reaction to alcohol is significantly affected by his or her expectations.*

placebo) —were rated by observers as less anxious, and exhibited less physiological arousal (exhibited slower heart rates) during the social interaction. The men who believed they had consumed alcoholic beverages also reported having experienced less anxiety while with the woman than those who thought they had drunk only tonic. In other words, for these college men just the belief that they had consumed alcohol was enough to reduce their social anxiety.

In fact, the findings showed that a few alcoholic drinks had no effect on social anxiety if the person did not know he had received them (active or anti-placebo). The results of this study support the theory that people's expectations about the effects of alcohol can greatly influence the changes in sociability experienced while drinking. This same conclusion can be drawn from later research on drinking and social anxiety in women, but with an interesting twist.

A second, similar balanced-placebo study involved female college students and examined their reactions when asked to make a good impression on an unfamiliar man. The results again showed that expectations influenced how the women felt, but in this case those who thought they had received alcoholic beverages (active or placebo) showed *more* signs of social anxiety than those who believed they had drunk only tonic (anti-placebo or control). Again, the alcohol itself had no direct effect on sociability.

The opposite response of men and women can be explained if one assumes that in this society drinking has a

This 19th-century advertisement employs Uncle Sam, the personification of America, to imply that because Kentucky Tavern Whiskey is accepted by and used in marine hospitals and soldiers homes, it should be the whiskey of choice of all truly patriotic citizens.

different "social meaning" for women and for men. Some people think drinking is not ladylike or that an intoxicated woman is inviting trouble when in unfamiliar situations. Thus, when a woman in this experiment thought she had consumed alcohol (active or placebo), she may have become worried that the man would disapprove of her or that she would have difficulty keeping a comfortable level of control in this interaction with a stranger. These feelings would naturally increase her level of anxiety.

In any case, the difference between the reactions of males and females in these studies only serves to highlight the role that socially learned expectations about alcohol play in the effects of drinking. It is too simple to think that alcohol directly causes all the changes seen in the social behavior of drinkers.

Contrary to the implications in this 1899 ad, all whiskey consumed in quantity will produce headaches and other hangover symptoms. When ads similar to this first appeared the temperance society countered them with notices carrying messages such as "God Gives us the only drink—'tis pure, cold water," and "Apples are God's bottles."

Sexual Reactions

Expectations about the effects of alcohol on sexuality have, if nothing else, a bit more colorful history than that associated with simple sociability. William Shakespeare wrote that where sexuality is concerned, drinking "provokes the desire, but it takes away the performance." And a more modern writer, Ogden Nash, has suggested that alcohol can be used to encourage women to respond more favorably to their partners' sexual advances in his comment "Candy is dandy, but liquor is quicker." The popular expectation seems to be that drinking will lead to more sexual activity, though it is unclear how actual sexual performance will be affected. Some argue that alcohol directly stimulates sexual activity, while others believe it anesthetizes, or deadens, the area of the brain that controls inhibitions and thus "releases" sexual impulses. But what do we really know about alcohol and sex?

One clear conclusion that can be drawn from available research is that doses of alcohol producing BACs of about 0.06% or greater can reduce the physiological sexual response in most people. This is probably due to the sedative or depressive action of alcohol on parts of the nervous system critical to sexual functioning. Higher levels of BAC often make it extremely difficult or even impossible for both males and females to experience normal sexual arousal and orgasm, as measured physiologically.

However, it is important to realize that sex is not just a physical response, but involves psychological aspects as well. People may need to overcome self-consciousness, inhibition, or guilt before they can participate in or enjoy sex— regardless of their physiological *potential* to respond. In fact, most clinical cases involving sexual problems do not involve any physical defects in the patients' bodies, but rather psychological complications, which may include the patients' lack of comfort concerning sex. These kinds of psychological factors are similar to expectations, and so it is interesting and beneficial to examine how people's beliefs about drinking and sex influence their reactions.

In the first balanced-placebo study of drinking and sexuality, male volunteers were first given several drinks which they thought contained either vodka and tonic or tonic water alone, though the actual contents of the beverages were sometimes different from those expected. Thus, the part played by alcohol and expectations in determining changes in sexual responses could be separated and better understood. After drinking, each man was taken to a private room where he was left alone to hook up a special device for measuring erections of the penis. He then viewed a series of brief films containing nudity and explicit sexual scenes.

The results of the physical measure of sexual response, as well as the men's later reports of how stimulated they had felt during the films, showed that alcohol itself had no effect. However, the men who believed they had consumed vodka drinks (active or placebo) showed significantly more sexual arousal than those who thought they had received only tonic (anti-placebo or control). The expectations about drinking alcohol apparently were enough to change not only the personal feelings of the men, but also the way their bodies responded to sexual stimuli.

In another similar study, the sexual materials the men viewed included three types of videotaped scenes: (1) of a man's normal sexual relation with a woman; (2) of the forcible rape of a woman; and (3) of the brutal beating of a

A well-dressed man (seated at left) contemplates investigating an "adult" bookstore in Los Angeles. Balanced-placebo studies have found that, no matter what substance they actually drink, men who believe they have consumed alcohol feel less restrained about enjoying erotic materials than men who think they have consumed a nonalcoholic beverage.

woman. The remarkable finding was that men who thought they had been drinking alcohol—regardless of what they actually had received (active or placebo) —were more likely to become aroused by the rape and violence scenes than men who believed they had nonalcoholic beverages (anti-placebo or control). It seemed that the expectations about alcohol, though not the alcohol itself, led the men to feel less restrained or more sexually responsive to scenes of deviant sexual behavior and even violence against women, as well as to ordinary erotic materials like those in the previous experiment.

A third balanced-placebo study of males attempted to explore the apparent "permission-giving" function of drinking where sexual behavior is concerned. In this experiment all the men took a special personality test designed to measure how much guilt they generally had about sex. They

In a bar in Washington, D.C., a customer dancing on the counter exhibits the loss of inhibitions that often accompanies drinking.

then received drinks as in the other studies and were given an opportunity to view a series of slides of sexually explicit scenes. Again, those who thought they had been drinking alcohol (active or placebo) reported greater sexual arousal than the others, no matter what they had actually received.

The most interesting finding, however, was that the men with a high level of guilt about sex who believed they had consumed alcohol (active or placebo) eagerly looked at the slides for a longer time than the others. The expectation associated with alcohol gave permission or served as an excuse for what otherwise one would expect to have been restrained behavior. In this case, it was harmless enough, but the more accepting attitude toward rape associated with drinking in the previous study could be dangerous.

Another balanced-placebo experiment looked at how females' sexual reactions changed while drinking. Following the usual procedures, women viewed films of sexual activity while a special instrument measured the physical changes in the vagina associated with sexual arousal. In addition, participants later described their sexual feelings. The results were a bit more complicated than those obtained for men. The more intoxicated the women said they felt, regardless of beverage received (active or placebo), the more sexual feelings they reported. However, the direct measurement of their vaginas indicated their bodies were actually less sexually aroused when they received alcohol (active or anti-placebo) than when they did not (placebo or control), no matter what drinks they believed they had gotten. Thus, expectations did not affect the women's physiological responses (though they were reduced by alcohol), even if the expectations did lead to a greater psychological sense of sexuality in those who *thought* they were intoxicated.

It is unclear why in these kinds of experiments males and females do not respond in the same way. Perhaps women have less drinking experience and/or are less certain of the association between drinking and sexuality, so their expectations are not as strong. Or maybe it is easier for them to confuse feelings of intoxication with feelings of sexual arousal. It is clear from these studies that many sexual reactions and behaviors of people while drinking may be due to expectations, associations, and environmental cues, rather than from the direct action of alcohol.

Aggression

Aggression is one of the social consequences frequently associated with alcohol consumption. In fact, studies of arrest and prison records show that as many as 30% to 60% of all assaults, rapes, and murders involve drinking. For adolescents percentages run even higher. Given these facts, it is easy to conclude that alcohol directly causes aggressive behavior. Some have assumed that alcohol triggers violence through some as yet undiscovered effect on the brain. Others have argued that human beings have a natural aggressive drive or impulse that is usually restrained by guilt, fear, or social morals or laws, but can be "disinhibited" or "released" by alcohol as it tranquilizes or deadens an area of the brain supposedly responsible for self-control. Still others have suggested that alcohol directly stimulates feelings of power and the need to dominate, and that such effects make aggression more likely.

All these theories have two things in common: (1) They assume that alcohol either releases or causes aggression through a direct physiological action; and (2) they have received little scientific support, though they continue to be popular.

One balanced-placebo study tried to distinguish between the physiological and the psychological, or expected, effects while examining the relation between drinking and human aggression. For this study experimenters recruited a group of men who were heavy social drinkers. Half of them received plain tonic drinks, while half were given enough vodka and tonic to reach a BAC of .10%. Again, some of the men in each drinking group were misinformed about the real contents of their drinks (placebo or anti-placebo) so the effects of expectations or behavior could be tested. Remarkably, only a few of the men who actually received the large doses of alcohol when expecting only tonic (anti-placebo) reported strong suspicion that they had been misinformed.

After drinking, each participant interacted with another man trained to be either insulting (to provoke the subject) or neutral and friendly (to avoid provoking the subject). Then the two men were instructed how to perform a specific task which gave the participant an opportunity to be aggressive by punishing his partner whenever mistakes were made. Participants could choose from a series of buttons they had been told delivered different strength electric shocks to their partners. (Though partners were told to act pained, they did not actually get any shocks.) Thus, it was possible to compare what each participant thought he had drunk with what each one actually had drunk and see how his expectations affected his aggressiveness, as measured by the strength and length of the shocks with which he chose to punish his partner.

The main results of this study, illustrated in Figure 4, provided strong evidence that expectations about alcohol (i.e., the *belief* that one has been drinking) can influence aggressive behavior. In contrast, actual consumption of alcohol had no effect on aggression. Whether the subjects were provoked or not provoked by their partners, they were

Shootouts, common in the Old West frontier saloons, were probably as much due to lawlessness as to alcohol-produced aggression.

likely to give stronger and also longer shocks if they believed they had consumed vodka than if they thought they had drunk only tonic. Interestingly, measurement of the participants' reaction times in the same experiment showed that alcohol slowed the men's responses regardless of expectations.

Apparently beliefs about drinking had an effect on aggression, which, like other complex social behaviors, depends on a combination of the person's psychology, his or her social situation, and the social meaning of drinking and its cues. A simple physical behavior such as reaction time, on the other hand, is more likely to be affected by the direct physiological action of alcohol, regardless of expectations.

Some other studies of drinking and aggression do suggest that alcohol itself directly affects the likelihood of violence. For instance, if alcohol disturbs one's ability to think clearly and to interpret correctly the intentions behind other people's actions, then alcohol consumption could lead to an increased number of misunderstandings which could lead to hostility. It is also possible that violence accompanies drinking because alcohol decreases sensitivity to pain so that the intoxicated person will continue to be aggressive before concern about being hurt deters the aggressor. Nevertheless, the importance of the learned social meaning of alcohol as a cue for aggression and as an acceptable excuse for

Policemen in New York City's Madison Square Garden attempt to break up a free-for-all among beer-drinking basketball fans. Outbreaks of aggression at sports events are probably triggered by a combination of excessive alcohol consumption, and the highly charged, competitive atmosphere.

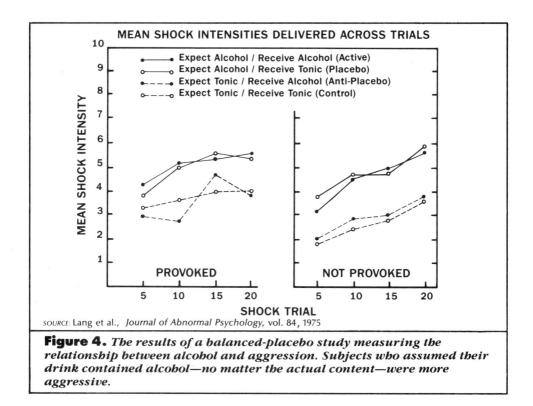

Figure 4. *The results of a balanced-placebo study measuring the relationship between alcohol and aggression. Subjects who assumed their drink contained alcohol—no matter the actual content—were more aggressive.*

antisocial behavior should be evident. Our society tends to expect more aggression from those who are intoxicated, and it also seems to be more tolerant of aggression exhibited by those who are drinking. This cannot help but make a person more inclined and more free to express aggression when consuming alcohol, no matter how drunk he or she actually is.

Alcohol alone does not cause aggression, and probably has little or no direct effect on it. Finally, this is supported by the simple observation that drinking frequently occurs without causing even the slightest hint of aggression. Other factors must be involved, and surely beliefs and expectations are among them.

Conclusion

It should now be clear that many of the associations between drinking and behavior are at least partially learned, rather than a result of the direct and specific effects of alcohol. Alcohol can alter one's state of consciousness—dull the senses, cloud thinking, and impair movement—but the drinker and his or her environment must help determine what these alterations mean in terms of observable social behavior. Furthermore, it is a person's exposure to drinking and the social reactions to drinking which teaches him or her how to make these interpretations.

Considering all these factors, it appears that one of the key messages conveyed about alcohol in this society is that people have less control of their social behavior when drinking. Because of this widely accepted belief, one may feel that he or she does not have to take the responsibility for actions which, in turn, may lead to greater risk taking and less worry about the consequences. "I was drinking" seems such a convenient explanation or justification for any less than pleasant outcomes of drinking. This response is particularly attractive in areas of uncertainty about sociability or sexuality, where one's self-esteem is on the line.

Maybe when drinking you feel you can dance better or can be more at ease in conversation since you have a ready excuse for a missed step or dumb remark. Flirting and more direct sexual advances might also be less awkward or inhibited if you can blame any undesirable results on alcohol. Even trying to prove yourself in a fight or getting revenge through aggression is easier because if you lose or get caught you can always blame alcohol. Obviously, then, drinking can serve a social, psychological function with respect to important social behaviors, and this probably increases its association with them. If an association or behavior is rewarded, it will tend to become stronger and more frequent.

Despite the psychological attractiveness of drinking's "excuse value," people do not always use alcohol nor is their behavior very much altered when they do drink in social situations. Some have enough confidence in their social skills, their sexuality, and their interpersonal strength that they are not likely to rely on alcohol to explain any potential shortcomings.

During the teenage years, however, young people, just forming their identities, try many new social behaviors, and the appeal of drinking to ease the trials may be especially great. Even if people do not plan to drink with the idea that it will make social risk taking easier, this is often the motiva-

tion behind their actions anyway. Almost without our awareness, the social meaning of drinking and the environmental
cues in the particular situation can change our behavior as
well as our responses to the way others act. This is a very
natural and very real phenomenon which reflects what our
society has taught us to expect about drinking.

The knowledge that these expected effects are largely
learned and not due to the direct physiological action of
alcohol represents a first step in the effort to change the
social meaning of drinking and minimize the potentially
destructive effects of the excusable irresponsibility with
which it has become associated. Society is a great educator,
successful in teaching what it sets out to teach. Unless it
makes the effort to spread a new image of drinking and the
drinker, the negative consequences associated with alcohol
use will persist.

*Assuring an alcohol-clinic patient that he is "not the first" to have a
drinking problem, a priest displays a cartoon of a man with a red nose, a
symptom commonly associated with alcoholism.*

A young derelict and his companions share a bottle of wine on a Denver, Colorado, street corner. Recent surveys show that the average age of the nation's skid row residents (95% of whom are male) is steadily dropping.

CHAPTER 6

PATTERNS OF ALCOHOL CONSUMPTION

Given what we now know about the physical, psychological, and social effects of alcohol consumption, it is instructive to examine patterns of drinking in this society. Who drinks and when did they start? How often and how much do they drink? What personal and environmental factors help determine differences in drinking patterns? What are the trends in American drinking? These questions will all be addressed in this chapter, with particular emphasis on the patterns of alcohol consumption in teenagers.

The existence of minimum drinking age laws suggest that youthful drinking is a major concern. But is this special attention warranted? Every society has the right and responsibility to protect its next generation from any unique risks presented by its inexperience. Is the level of teenage drinking and teenage drinking problems (see Chapter 7) out of line with the rest of society? One key point is that, while teenage drinking is a serious and probably growing danger, alcohol consumption and the alcohol-related problems of adults are undoubtedly more severe. Thus, while the focus on youth may represent a genuine desire to spare them from harm, it also reflects our society's ambivalence about alcohol.

Society tends to single out young people when it tries to control access to products and behaviors surrounded by moral ambiguity or uncertainty. Besides alcohol and drinking, the right to purchase contraceptives and the right to consent to sexual intercourse are examples of other controversial moral areas often subject to minimum age restrictions. Education and the modeling of responsible behavior would seem more effective than reliance on official restrictions which breed disrespect for the law and may even increase the attractiveness of the "forbidden fruits."

Many of our problems with alcohol probably exist because members of this society cannot agree on what stand to take regarding drinking by *anyone,* and so it is easier just to try to deny alcohol to youth. Unfortunately, this approach is not very effective and may also have negative consequences of its own. Not the least of these potential problems is that teenagers may come to see drinking as a symbol of being grown-up, even though there is little legitimate reason it should be associated with maturity, independence, power, or anything that being grown-up may represent.

Estimating Alcohol Consumption Rates

While rates of drinking in United States history have changed frequently, it is difficult to measure these changes precisely. At different points in history, social and economic factors may cause shifts in beverage preferences as well as in the proportion of the population who drink and how much alcohol they consume. For instance, during the latter part of the expansionary period (1780s to 1920) when the temperance movement was gaining strength, there was a general decline in drinking, especially drinking of hard liquor. The exact nature of these kinds of changes, however, can only be roughly estimated.

One method, called "apparent consumption" estimation, depends on reports of alcoholic beverage sales provided by states, taxing agencies, and the alcohol industry. The total amount of ethanol contained in beverages sold or distributed is then divided by the total population of potential drinkers (usually considered to be those at least 14 years or older) to arrive at an estimate of per capita (average per person) consumption for any particular year.

Based on this method, it appears that the average American drinks about 2.7 gallons of ethanol per year. That is about two drinks per day, every day! Obviously, the figure is even higher if abstainers (almost one-third of the adult population) are not counted. These averages, however, can be very misleading since it has been estimated that as few as 10% of adults are responsible for half of all alcohol consumption, thus reducing the averages for other adults considerably. Nonetheless, apparent consumption figures indicate that per capita alcohol consumption has been rising relatively slowly in recent years (about 1% per year since 1970, compared to 2% or 3% per year in the 1960s). It is also clear that beer is the most common source of alcohol, followed closely by distilled spirits, and finally by wine, which is growing in popularity.

In addition to the apparent consumption method, the other main approach to estimating drinking behavior is through surveys, which depend on the cooperation and self-reports of participants. Though the most widely used source of information, survey data may not provide accurate drinking estimates for the population. Because participants tend to misreport actual consumption (either they forget or do not choose to be honest about their drinking) and because the heaviest drinkers and those with the most problems often do not receive or complete survey questionnaires, alcohol use is usually underestimated. In fact, self-report

Scarce in the war years, scotch poured into the nation in the late 1940s.

figures account for only about half of the alcohol consumption that would be expected using the apparent consumption method.

Nevertheless, surveys are the only practical way to get detailed personal information associated with drinking and so they are relied on heavily. The best available recent survey of teenage drinking patterns is the Research Triangle Institute's 1978 study of almost 5,000 10th- through 12th-grade students representative of all areas of the United States. This study, as well as earlier work using 7th- through 12th-graders, served as the basis of much of what follows.

Patterns of Teenage Drinking

The first task in describing teenage drinking is to identify its beginnings, the proportion of teenagers who participate, the frequency and quantity of alcohol consumption, and the trends in these figures. By examining these data, especially in relation to drinking by adults, one should be able to determine whether or not a serious problem exists.

Surveys conducted in 1981 asked high school seniors to report the age at which they first used alcohol. More than half indicated that they had already done some drinking *before* entering high school (10th grade). It is unclear what the nature of this experience was—perhaps only a few sips at home—but the high rate of exposure indicates ample opportunity for experimentation with alcohol, despite minimum drinking age laws. By the senior year in high school more than 9 out of 10 students said they had tried alcohol, and fully 80% of 10th through 12th graders had used alco-

In 1973 teenagers in Dallas, Texas, celebrated the lowering of the drinking age to 18. Though young people tend to drink less regularly than older people, when they do drink they usually consume greater quantities.

Table 4

	1978 National Survey of the Drinking Patterns of 4,918 High School Students	
% OF TOTAL	DRINKING RATE CATEGORY
25.0	ABSTAINERS don't drink or drink less often than once a year.*
7.6	INFREQUENT DRINKERS drink once a month at most and drink small amounts per typical drinking occasion.**
18.8	LIGHT DRINKERS drink once a month at most and drink medium amounts per typical drinking occasion or drink no more than three to four times a month and drink small amounts per typical drinking occasion.
16.6	MODERATE DRINKERS drink at least once a week and small amounts per typical drinking occasion or three to four times a month and medium amounts per typical drinking occasion or no more than once a month and large amounts per typical drinking occasion.
17.3	MODERATE/HEAVIER DRINKERS drink at least once a week and medium amounts per typical drinking occasion or three to four times a month and large amounts per typical drinking occasion.
14.8	HEAVIER DRINKERS drink at least once a week and large amounts per typical drinking occasion.

*Those who drink less than once a year were classified as abstainers because the absolute alcohol consumed per day was essentially nil. Of those classified as abstainers above, 4.0% were former drinkers; i.e., they had had at least two or three drinks at some time in the past but not in the preceding year.

**Small, medium, and large amounts refer to one drink or less per drinking occasion, two to four drinks per drinking occasion, and five or more drinks per drinking occasion, respectively. For this survey a drink meant 12 oz. of beer, 4 oz. of wine, or 1 oz. of distilled spirits.

SOURCE: Adapted from Rachal et al., NIAAA, *Alcohol and Health Monograph*, No.1, 1982.

hol in the past year. In addition, evidence from several studies showed that the proportion of teenagers who have used alcoholic beverages has not changed much since the mid-1970s, though it rose steadily from the 1940s through the 1960s.

Merely trying alcoholic beverages and actually drinking heavily, however, are two very different things. To create a better picture of rates of drinking behavior, researchers have developed classifications of drinkers based on the frequency of drinking occasions and the average quantity consumed during each occasion. These descriptive classifications are detailed in Table 4 along with the percentages of high school students who fell into each category in a 1978 survey.

While more than half of the students were classified as nondrinkers, infrequent drinkers, or light drinkers, the remainder (48.7%) could be considered at least "regular" drinkers. Perhaps more important, almost 15% of these high school students fit in the heavier drinking category. A comparison of this survey with data available from earlier studies shows that there has been little change in teenage drinking since 1974.

A comparison of the proportions and rates of teenage drinking with those of persons over 18 years old provides some interesting results. A smaller percentage of teenagers than adults, especially older adults, could be classed as abstainers. This probably reflects greater experimentation by young people. Data on rates of drinking, however, showed that the heaviest alcohol consumption occurs in young adults (age 21–34) and peaks in the mid 20s. In general, an examination of drinking by age indicates that rates show a rather orderly increase through adolescence and into the 20s, rather than any abrupt changes due to the legality or acceptability of drinking associated with any particular age. After peaking, there is also a gradual trend toward fewer drinkers (espe-

Students from Trenton State College in New Jersey demonstrate against a proposal to raise the state's drinking age to 21. The slogan on the poster clearly illustrates the type of mixed message that lawmakers often give teenagers—a 19-year-old is mature enough to defend his or her country, but too immature to drink. Inconsistencies such as this work against the drive to educate people about drugs and drug abuse.

cially fewer heavy drinkers) and lower overall rates of consumption during the older adult years. A reasonable conclusion would be that teenage drinking is seen as just part of growing up, part of the transition into the first stage of adulthood.

Factors Influencing Teenage Alcohol Use

Too much has been made of the argument that teenage drinking is largely an act of rebellion against society or parents. Unlike many psychoactive drugs, alcohol is accepted in this society, and therefore teenage drinking might reflect more of a desire to share in the experiences of adult society than to rebel against its values. Similarly, most parents drink and often do not set clear guidelines for alcohol use by their children, so teenage drinking could be more a response to a lack of limitations rather than outright rebellion.

Most teenagers' self-reported reasons for alcohol use are not much different from those given by older drinkers. They emphasize positive expectations of increased pleasure in a variety of experiences. Little mention is made of rebellion, and few members of either group list escape from or compensation for specific negative states of the individual (e.g., restriction, boredom, anxiety, loneliness, etc.). Finally, the patterns of alcohol use by both the young and adults are influenced by a number of factors, though the average drinker may be unaware of, or at least relatively uninterested in them. These are summarized below as they apply to teenagers.

Age Among the uncontrollable factors with which you must live is your age, and probably the most consistent finding of research on adolescent drinking involves age. The older the teenager the more likely he or she is to use alcoholic beverages, and the more likely the rate of alcohol consumption will be high. Available evidence indicates that adolescent drinking increases most between the ages of 13 and 15. Such age-related changes are most apparent in extreme categories of drinking rates as shown by a 1974 survey. Whereas at age 13 over 60% of those surveyed fit the abstainer or infrequent drinker descriptions and only about 10% fit the moderate/heavier or heavier categories, by age 15 only one-third were in the lower groups and almost 30% were in the higher ones.

Gender Gender is (for the most part) another unchangeable factor associated with drinking patterns. While at least 70% of high school girls have done some drinking, 1978 survey data showed that significantly higher proportions of boys than girls use alcohol, and that males typically drink at higher rates than females across all age groups. As with age, gender differences are more evident at extremes of drinking rates. Among high schoolers, 40% of boys and only 25% of girls fit the two highest drinking-rate categories (moderate/ heavier and heavier). Even this difference, however, is not as great as it has been in past years. The trend seems to be toward more similarity in the drinking behaviors of the sexes. Indeed, it may be that among teenagers who do drink, girls already approximate boys in terms of the average BACs they reach while drinking since their generally lower body weight means females typically have to consume less alcohol to reach the same level of intoxication.

Race The last important, unmodifiable drinking influence is race. The largest difference here is that among teenagers there are many more blacks than whites in the abstainer and lighter-drinking categories, but the reverse is true for the moderate- to heavier-drinking groups. Hispanics have drinking patterns more similar to whites than to blacks, though few report drinking rates that would place them in the heaviest drinking category.

The family The family, and particularly one's parents, has the potential to exert great influence on teenage drinking. Parents determine where the family will live, and drinking habits are associated with region of the country (for example, there are many more abstainers in the South than in the Northeast) and size of the community (for example, there is more drinking in urban than rural areas), though these differences are small and decreasing.

Children often share their parents' religion and this, too, is relevant to alcohol use. Catholic teenagers drink slightly more than other groups, and Protestants are more likely to abstain than Jews. Even family structure (e.g., absence of one or both parents, family size, birth order) and general family relations (e.g., discipline practices, closeness, degree of negativity) have been shown to have some connection with drinking by teenage family members. For instance, there is more alcohol use by youths in homes where a parent is absent and/or family relations are strained. The family-related factors that show the greatest relation to adolescent drinking, however, are parental attitudes about teenage drinking and the parents' own drinking behavior.

Parental influence on children's drinking can take at least two important forms. The first is verbal instruction and the establishment and enforcement of rules or standards. This is the aspect of parenting that directly communicates approval or disapproval of the youth's drinking. Its impact is greatest for younger children and fades as they age. The second type of influence is parental modeling of drinking behavior. In both of these forms of influence parents can be either consistent ("Do as I say and as I do.") or inconsistent ("Do as I say, not as I do."). In general, research shows that rates of teenage alcohol use increase as the degree of parental approval of it increases. It is interesting, however, that extreme disapproval by parents has been associated with some of the heaviest teenage drinking. This may be an illustration of one instance of drinking as a form of rebellion or a search for the "forbidden fruit."

A 1904 advertisement which subtly illustrates the proper etiquette of drinking with dinner—male family members enjoy ale while the lady of the house abstains. Lifelong drinking practices are often formed within the family unit, and the drinking behavior of parents frequently determines their children's drinking patterns.

Parent's own drinking habits also are paralleled fairly closely by those of their teenage children, though again there are some exceptions. In this case, the heavy teenage drinkers do not necessarily perceive their parents to be heavy drinkers as well. The overall role of family factors influencing drinking diminishes as the child gets older.

Peers Many authorities on teenage drinking have emphasized the special role of peer influences in alcohol use by young people. Unfortunately, peer influences often have not been precisely defined. Moreover, if one carefully examines the importance of social conformity in adult drinking, it is clear that observation of others and failure to exercise self-control contribute heavily to the drinking (and especially overdrinking) of this group as well. Several laboratory experiments have shown that the presence of a heavy-drinking model leads to heavier alcohol consumption by adults (aged 21 and up), and that the imitation is greatest when the model is most like the subject in terms of important personal characteristics. Thus, it appears that peer influences are by no means unique to teenagers and their drinking. But just what is the relation between teenage drinking and peers?

Peer influences include peer pressure (direct encouragement to drink and/or drinking that is motivated by a

A mother yells at her husband about their alcoholic son (center) in an improvised scene presented by Awareness Theater of Rochester, New York. By dramatizing family problems the theater company hopes to improve understanding and communication between teenagers and their families.

desire to be accepted or approved), peer attitudes about drinking, and actual drinking behavior by peers. Surveys of teenagers indicated that few report that direct peer pressure is important in their alcohol use decisions, though encouragement to drink may be more of a factor in initial use and among heavier drinkers. Less obvious peer influences, operating through general attitudes and drinking behavior, do seem to be critical for most young people. A teenager's drinking experience and rate are probably best predicted by knowing how many of his or her friends drink, how much they drink and how much he or she approves of their drinking.

In the 1978 national high school survey it was shown that more than half of the students who had two or fewer friends who drank were themselves abstainers. On the other hand, if most or all of a student's peers were drinkers, then the chances were 7 in 10 that he or she was *at least* a moderate drinker. As for perception of peer approval, survey results showed that half of 10th- through 12th-graders think peers approve of drinking, and nearly as many believe they are neutral on the issue. Less than 10% thought peers disapproved, and there was a close association between rate of drinking and perceived level of peer approval for it. Overall, it appears that parents' concerns about their children "getting in with the wrong crowd" are well founded and the importance of peer influences in teenage drinking probably increases with age.

Social and Physical Context As noted earlier, both the social situation and the physical surrounding can influence drinking behavior. From the social perspective, teenage drinking companions are peers or friends about twice as often as they are parents or other relatives. Few young people report drinking alone very often. The heavier the drinking the more likely it is to be with peers, though those who do most of their drinking alone do so with higher frequency and in larger quantities. The home is the single most common setting for drinking, but the majority of alcohol consumption—especially heavier drinking—takes place in locations (bars, cars, outside, etc.) outside the home. In sum, the most popular context for heavy drinking is with peers somewhere other than at home.

Personality, Values and Activities Although, in general, personality factors and values are only weakly related to level of drinking, some of them do predict initiation or age of onset of drinking and later problems with alcohol. Among these are a high tolerance of deviance in others, a high value placed on independence rather than academic achievement (where little success is expected), and a low commitment to religion. Perhaps surprising is the fact that level of alcohol use is *not* at all strongly associated with participation in school, social activities, or even academic achievement. However, the heaviest drinkers in the 1978 high school survey were far more likely to get the lowest than the highest grades. With respect to marijuana and other drugs, heavy drinkers also were more likely than alcohol abstainers to use other psychoactive substances.

Conclusion

This brief review of patterns of teenage drinking and the factors influencing them suggests several conclusions. The first is that alcohol is the most widely used drug in America by young and old alike. It is highly available and its use is

The Seagram liquor company sponsored the advertisements on these two pages, claiming that "the interests of both the company and the consumer are best served by the moderate use of distilled spirits." Through ads such as these the company hopes to present itself as being concerned about public health and the risks of alcohol abuse. However, nowhere do these ads report the fact that alcohol is a drug that can cause addiction and serious physiological damage.

generally accepted, so teenagers have more than ample opportunity to try it. The second point is that in this society drinking is a learned behavior that is seen as part of normal development and transition into adulthood. Like many other important learned behaviors, drinking level is a response to a complex set of personal and environmental factors whose influence may vary at different ages. Among the most significant of these factors identified so far are parents and peers.

Finally, it is worth noting that the levels of teenage drinking have not increased any faster than the drinking by members of other age groups in recent years. This is not to say that drinking problems in young people are insignificant. However, focusing on teenage drinking, while the equally or even more serious alcohol problems of the adult population persist, underlines this society's ambivalence about drinking. In the long run such continued inconsistency and ambiguity, including the unintentional equating of alcohol use with maturity, independence, and power, can only be counterproductive to dealing successfully with alcohol abuse and its problems.

When he was six years old Joel Maker had to give up smoking and drinking in order to enter kindergarten. His father had also been addicted to alcohol but graduated from an alcohol treatment center.

CHAPTER 7

THE DRINKING PROBLEMS OF TEENAGERS

*A*s established in the previous chapter, some alcohol use is normative behavior for United States teenagers —the majority of young people drink regardless of the official rules of society which prohibit it. But how many teenagers *misuse* alcohol, what is the nature of their drinking problems, who are they, and what factors can help us to predict such difficulties? These questions will be addressed in the present chapter. First, however, the meaning of alcohol misuse or problem drinking must be clarified.

Concepts and Definitions of Problem Drinking

Alcoholism, in general, and teenage alcoholism, in particular, have received considerable attention in the popular media. Unfortunately, these terms have very little meaning because they have been carelessly applied to so many different kinds of drinking habits, patterns, and consequences. For the most part, however, use of the label "alcoholic" implies that drinking problems should be understood in terms of a disease (see Chapter 1). In this sense, the alcoholic usually is regarded as being biologically different with respect to his or her reactions to alcohol, and presumably this is a difference in the nature or quality of the response, not just the degree or quantity of drinking problems.

Two additional key assumptions of the traditional disease concept of alcoholism are that (1) for physiological reasons the abstaining alcoholic will crave alcohol and will be unable to control his or her drinking once the first drink is consumed, and (2) problems with alcohol represent a progressive and irreversible disorder which will only get worse with time unless all drinking is stopped.

Scientific evidence that provides *unqualified* support for the disease concept for all alcoholics is extremely scarce, and results of many studies challenge its assumptions. Genetic research has established that children of alcoholics have a greater chance of developing drinking problems than

children of nonalcoholics, supposedly due to the similarity of parents' and their children's genes. If one of a pair of identical twins is an alcoholic, his co-twin, who has identical genes, is more likely to be alcoholic than is the case for fraternal twins, who are no more genetically alike than non-twin siblings. However, many children of alcoholics have no drinking problems, and of identical twins born to alcoholics, one twin may have drinking problems while the other may not. Furthermore, although persons from alcoholic families have more than their share of alcohol problems, most people with serious alcohol problems do not have a clear family history of similar difficulties. Thus, while heredity surely does play a role in one's susceptibility to drinking problems, it is probably not the whole story.

Similar conclusions can be drawn from research attempting to establish a specific and acquired biological difference between alcoholics and nonalcoholics to explain reactions to alcohol. Though some physical changes are a result of continued heavy drinking (see Chapter 4), none of these, such as allergic reactions or a defective metabolism, has proven to be either necessary or sufficient to explain alcoholism. In fact, most bodily differences in people with different levels of drinking are more a matter of degree than an all-or-none type of characteristic. This is clearly the case where tolerance is concerned, to give just one example.

Assumptions about a physiological basis for an alcoholic's craving and/or "loss-of-control drinking" after a period of sobriety not only lack research support, but have actually been contradicted by much of the available data. Certainly, many people with a history of heavy drinking frequently desire alcohol and after taking a first drink may appear to be unable to stop. That is not the issue. The question is, What causes these feelings and behaviors? If they are based strictly on physical reactions, then they might be expected to occur continuously and without exception. However, problem drinkers report that craving varies depending on their psychological state and a variety of environmental factors.

Research has also shown that diagnosed "alcoholics" do not always lose control of their drinking when receiving alcohol. For instance, laboratory studies on the role of expectations in loss-of-control drinking have demonstrated that alcoholics will drink more when they think their beverages contain alcohol (regardless of the actual contents) than when they think the drinks are nonalcoholic (even if they do contain alcohol). And hospital research has shown that alcoholics given free access to alcohol do not always get drunk after each time they start drinking, and that they are capable of voluntarily cutting down their consumption if they are immediately rewarded or can avoid punishment by doing so. Finally, there are documented cases in which alcoholics have reduced their alcohol consumption and continued social drinking for extended periods of time ranging up to many years.

This last finding questions the belief that if you experience drinking problems this means you are suffering from a progressive, irreversible disorder which always gets worse with continued use of alcohol. Some diagnosed alcoholics have learned to control their drinking without total abstinence. However, just because an alcoholic stops drinking does not mean all of his or her problems (whether physical

Previously it was not unreasonable to predict that any teenager with a drinking problem would most likely end up like these drunks near Times Square, New York City. But today, because of more accurate information about alcohol and more sophisticated therapeutic techniques, youth counselors can offer more positive futures.

or psychological) will disappear. As long as the problems persist, the urge to "solve" them by drinking will also.

It is simplest and most sensible for problem drinkers to stop using alcohol altogether. For many, total abstinence is the only way to prevent uncontrollable drinking. But this does not mean that drinking problems will *necessarily* get worse if one does not quit, as is maintained by the disease concept of alcoholism. In fact, research that has followed the same people from their college years through middle age has found that one's early level of drinking (including problem drinking) is not a very good predictor of his or her later level of alcohol consumption or related problems. This is critical information where teenagers are concerned, since it is often assumed that problem drinking during adolescence means one is condemned to a life of alcoholism. There is little evidence to support this assumption.

If "alcoholism," as described by the traditional disease concept, is a poor way of defining drinking problems, what is the alternative? Firstly, a good definition should not place too much emphasis on alcohol consumption alone. Everyone has heard stories of very old, but healthy and well-adjusted, persons telling of how they have drunk alcohol nearly every day for most of their lives and it did them no harm. These, of course, may be exceptional cases, since long-term heavy drinking has been shown to cause serious physical damage. However, drinking problems should be defined not just by the drinking itself, but in terms of their *consequences.* Among the important life areas that might be affected by alcohol use and which should be considered are social relations, school or job functioning, and legal involvement, as well as physical health.

Secondly, a good definition of problem drinking must allow for different levels of severity. People do not either have or not have problems with alcohol, but instead the problems exist to different degrees. Skipping school several times a week to drink and drive around vandalizing and getting into fights is obviously a worse problem than drinking too much at a party a few months ago, though both are alcohol-related problems.

Finally, a definition of problem drinking is most useful if it focuses on the here-and-now. It should emphasize the difficulties that alcohol use causes or can cause the person today or in the near future. It is generally not useful or helpful to try to guess whether a current drinking problem means a person will become an alcoholic. With our present knowledge it would only be guesswork, anyway, especially when it is unclear what being an "alcoholic" really means.

Prevalence of Teenage Drinking Problems

Defining the drinking problems of teenagers is more complicated than doing so for the adult population for several reasons. Firstly, for most teenagers between the age of 13 and 17 (and in most states everyone up to the age of 21) use of alcoholic beverages is illegal. Because of this, any use of alcohol could be considered to be an alcohol-related problem. Secondly, since society does not expect as much of young people as it does of adults, nor does it give young people as many responsibilities, the effects of drinking may be more difficult to detect than they are in adults. For instance, most teenagers do not have to support themselves or a family, and thus if they lose a job due to drinking or lack money because they have spent it on alcohol, it would probably not appear to be as serious or obvious a consequence of problem drinking as a similar outcome would be for an adult breadwinner or homemaker.

Finally, since teenagers have had a shorter period of time and fewer opportunities to experience alcohol use, they consequently suffer less from the long-term effects of chronic, heavy drinking (especially the physically damaging effects) which often figure into the identification of older problem drinkers. Given these considerations, it is necessary that the definitions of problem drinking applied to teenagers be different from those applied to adults.

Several national surveys of teenagers have based their descriptions of problem drinking or alcohol misuse on two main factors: (1) frequency of self-reported drunkenness in the past year, and (2) past-year experiences of alcohol-related negative consequences in five areas: friends, dates, school, driving, and the police. Using these factors, problem drinking in teenagers is typically defined as a minimum of six episodes of drunkenness and/or at least two occasions of negative consequences in three or more of the five areas, during the past year.

In the best available surveys, the questions concerning the frequency of problems in the five areas during the past year included: How many times have you gotten into difficulties of any kind with your friends because of your drinking? How many times have you been criticized by someone you were dating because of your drinking? How many times have you gotten into trouble with your teachers or principal because of your drinking? How many times have you driven when you've had a lot to drink? How many times have you gotten into trouble with the police because of your drinking?

In 1978 about 31% of high school students (10th to 12th grade) could be labeled as alcohol misusers or problem drinkers, an increase from 27% in 1974. Approximately 90% of the problem drinkers identified in each survey were classified as such because of the frequency of their drunkenness rather than multiple negative consequences of drinking. There also seemed to be a trend toward more heavy drinking by teenagers from the earlier to the later survey.

While few high schoolers who misused alcohol had as many as two occasions of negative consequences in at least three areas, most (78% in 1974, and 69% in 1978) who had been drunk six or more times the previous year did experience *at least* one negative consequence because of their

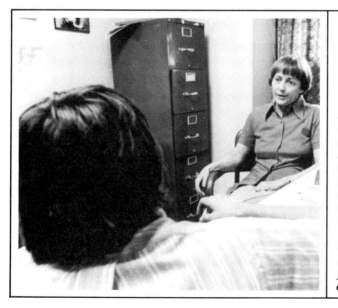

Dr. Joan Curlee-Salisbury talks with a teenager in her Indianapolis alcohol-treatment program. The psychologist told an interviewer that she likes alcoholics. "When they recover," she said, "they recover so beautifully. It's just amazing what nice people they turn out to be."

drinking. This was a much higher rate of unfavorable drinking-related outcomes than was found for teenagers who used alcohol but were not classified as misusers. Interestingly, few members of either group who did report negative consequences felt drinking had been a problem for them. Perhaps they confused problem drinking with the common image and definition of "alcoholism."

Factors Associated with Teenage Alcohol Misuse

Many of the factors associated with general teenage alcohol use (see Chapter 6) have also been studied with reference to teenagers who misuse alcohol or are problem drinkers. Age is one factor for which overall increases in rates of drinking are closely paralleled by increasing rates of problem drinking from earlier to later years of adolescence.

In the case of effects due to gender, however, the results show striking differences. It appears that the proportion of females with heavy drinking problems does not grow nearly as rapidly with age as it does for males. In fact, among high schoolers 15 years old or younger, 31% of males and 24% of females were classified as alcohol misusers. Yet for those age 18 and older, 44% of males and 25% of females fit the misuser category. Thus, in recent years while the prevalence of general alcohol use for teenage males and females has become more similar and these differences narrow across the high school years, the gap between male and female rates of alcohol *misuse* or problem drinking seems to widen considerably between 9th grade and graduation. Older teenage boys clearly experience the most alcohol problems.

In addition to age and sex differences, alcohol misuse among teenagers varies with several other less critical factors. For example, some studies show a higher rate of problem drinking among white teenagers than either blacks or Hispanics. And other minor differences have been found for region of the country (more misuse in Northeast and Northcentral areas than in the South), and religion (more misuse by Catholics than Protestants or Jews). However, the key factors that help distinguish the teenage abstainer and nonproblem drinker from the teenage problem drinker include environmental influences involving parents and peers.

Personality characteristics and personal values, though relatively unimportant in general alcohol use by young people, appear to play a larger role in alcohol misuse by this group.

Before summarizing parent, peer, and personality factors associated with teenage problem drinking (and, to a lesser extent, with later difficulties with alcohol in adult-

hood), it should be emphasized that no one factor or even any combination of them is necessary or sufficient for problems to occur. Their presence is only *correlated* with alcohol misuse. In other words, the specific environmental and personal characteristics simply *tend* to be present in cases of teenage problem drinking, though they may not actually *cause* or influence them in any particular instance. It is just that these factors and alcohol misuse are present simultaneously.

The parental characteristics and family factors associated with adolescent problem drinking include the following: (1) parents who are heavier drinkers themselves and who do not show much disapproval of drinking by their teenage children; (2) parents who show little involvement with their children, creating a family with little unity, affection, or general positive atmosphere; and (3) parents whose standards for their children's behavior and discipline patterns are inadequate or inconsistent, though not necessarily harsh.

The existence of the first factor, which is specific to drinking, seems to better predict teenage alcohol misuse than the more general family factors. However, it may be the lack of a close family with clear expectations (number 2) which leads the young person to be more strongly influenced by peers at an earlier age. In fact, as will become evident below, many of the peer factors associated with adolescent problem drinking are stated in a way which relates them to parental influences.

Among the peer factors associated with teenage alcohol misuse are: (1) peer approval of drinking and numerous peers who model a variety of problem behaviors, including problem drinking; (2) a perception on the part of the teenager of a relatively high level of disagreement between his or her parents and peers; and (3) an apparent willingness to be more influenced by peers than by parents at a fairly early age. Once again, the peer factors that directly pertain to drinking seem most critical, though there is some reason to believe that problem drinking teenagers choose friends who drink rather than drinking because their peers do.

Though the environmental impact of parents and peers is undoubtedly important in teenage problem drinking, researchers have identified a number of individual characteristics, including personality, temperament, attitudes, and values, which probably play a role as well. Compared to abstainers and nonproblem drinkers, young alcohol misusers: (1) place a higher value on independence from parents and other authorities; (2) expect less academic success and value such achievement less; (3) attach less importance to religion; (4) weigh the positive effects of drinking more heavily than the negative effects, perhaps partly because they have different physiological reactions to alcohol; and (5) show more tolerance of deviance in general, and may themselves be more liable to act on impulse and get involved in other problem behavior.

With respect to this last tendency, teenagers with drinking problems have been found to have above average rates of school problems (academic problems, behavior problems in the classroom, skipping classes or days of school, and dropout), early sexual involvement, use of marijuana and other illegal drugs, and general juvenile delinquency. Indeed, some experts see problem drinking as just one of a number of problem behaviors that represent some adoles-

A University of Maryland student puffs on a "joint" during a marijuana smoke-in. Teenagers with drinking problems also frequently use marijuana and other illegal drugs. Some researchers feel that this focus on drugs may represent a teenager's reaction to the stressful transition from childhood to adolescence.

cents' reactions to the stressful transition from childhood to adolescence. In the absence of positive parental influences, this transition may begin prematurely or be otherwise disturbed, making both problem drinking and other difficulties more likely.

Research has also shown that changes in drinking patterns often accompany other later transitions or life changes (e.g., marriage or separation/divorce, shifts in school or job status) and that drinking may become more of a problem at these points too. Thus, alcohol use may be seen as a potentially problematic part of the ongoing process of development throughout one's life.

In keeping with the theme of alcohol's involvement in developmental processes, the relation of drinking to initiation into other kinds of drug use should be mentioned. It is often said that using alcohol will lead to experimentation with other drugs, or that marijuana is a stepping-stone to heroin. In a study of white 14- to 18-year-olds in New York State high schools of the early 1970s, researchers questioned students at two different points in time to try to investigate which kinds of drug use came before others. They found that beer or wine was the first psychoactive substance which most people tried. The next was liquor or cigarettes, and third was marijuana. And only then came initiation into the use of other illicit (illegal for all ages) drugs such as cocaine, heroin, etc.

Reaching a point in this sequence does not necessarily mean you will go on to the next stage. But if you have reached a certain stage the chances are very good that you have at least passed through all the preceding stages in order. Thus, the majority (68%) of cigarette smokers in the survey had done some drinking, but only 21% of alcohol users smoked. Perhaps more important, nearly every illicit drug user had first tried marijuana, smoked cigarettes, and used all forms of alcoholic beverages.

This sequence may reflect a hierarchy of drug acceptability in our culture, differing levels of drug availability, degrees of tolerance for deviance associated with each stage, or some combination of these and other factors. There is some evidence to suggest that the younger one enters or starts the sequence, the more likely he or she is to complete it, with increased chances of problem drinking and other problems along the way.

Research on stages in drug use also calls attention to the high rate of poly- or multiple-drug use among drug abusers. In one survey of adolescents in substance abuse treatment, two-thirds used illicit drugs in combination with alcohol. This, of course, is a potentially dangerous combination because the actual contents of street drugs are unreliable and alcohol has synergistic interaction effects with many substances (see Chapter 3). Incidentally, 9 out of 10 of these teenagers with drug problems had used alcohol before starting on other substances.

Conclusion

There can be little doubt that as the most widely used drug, alcohol is also the most misused. Estimates of the proportion of teenage problem drinking, defined in terms of drunkenness and negative consequences, average around 30% for high school students. High school drinking problems seem to be worst among older teenagers (especially boys), and have been associated with approval and modeling of drinking by both parents and peers, with an atmosphere of poor parenting contributing to early and excessive dependence on peer relationships. The teenagers who misuse alcohol tend to reject traditional values, and act independently but impulsively, such that their behavior leads them to involvement with other problems, including the abuse of other drugs.

Clearly, the severity and diversity of problems associated with teenage drinking deserve attention. However, the modest, recent increases in teenage alcohol abuse do not exceed those evident in the adult population, where the overall rate and severity of consequences may be higher. The emphasis many alcohol abuse prevention and management efforts place on young people probably reflects society's ambivalence about attacking adult drinking problems head-on. What is most evident is the need for consistent messages and policies and a concerted effort to better understand each group's particular characteristics. All alcohol abusers deserve attention.

Members of the Sumner County Council, a Wellington, Kansas, alcoholic-rehabilitation group organized to rehabilitate the town's alcoholics, examine a brochure that reflects their philosophy about alcoholism—that problem drinking is a medical rather than a moral issue.

CHAPTER 8

ALCOHOL AND PUBLIC POLICY: THE MANAGEMENT AND PREVENTION OF DRINKING PROBLEMS

The disease concept of drinking problems, with its emphasis on treatment of alcoholics, has dominated American public policy related to alcohol for the last 50 years. While a subpopulation of alcoholics may have an abnormality as biologically-based as diabetes, many or most heavy drinkers are influenced by a mixture of social, emotional, and biological factors. Teenage drinkers are even more likely than adults to fall prey to damaging home or school circumstances. The disease concept fits nicely with this society's ambivalence about alcohol, and it has contributed to our inability to deal with drinking problems in an effective way.

Since Prohibition, Americans have resisted many specific government control efforts, especially those that interfere with modern consumerism and the drive for leisure and pleasure which replaced the traditional values of self-reliance dealt a blow by the Great Depression. In this atmosphere, the idea that most people should be free to determine their alcohol use was a natural one.

At the same time, professionals and self-help groups, such as Alcoholics Anonymous (AA), began gathering to discuss their special interest in determining why a small minority of drinkers consume extreme amounts of alcohol. They speculated about possible biological differences between normal drinkers and alcoholics.

The simple idea that alcohol problems arise from a poorly understood chemistry and the reaction between ethanol and certain drinkers' bodies seemed appealing. Moreover, it was a view that the general public was willing to support and accept, and one that did not offend the many diverse groups (the alcoholic beverage industry, restaurant associations, the legal profession, social service agencies, the medical establishment, AA, etc.) that might be affected by alcohol policies. Thus, the "alcoholism movement" was born.

Acceptance of the disease concept was probably also aided by a vocal group of recovered or "recovering" alcoholics who credited their success to treatments consistent with this simple model. The personal experiences reported by such victims of the presumed disease—however rare and unrepresentative of general alcohol problems they may have been—had (and often still have) a strong influence on the mind of the average person. Such opinions, not demonstrated facts, have helped shape public policy on alcohol to this day.

Through the late 1970s it is estimated that 80% of federal funds for alcohol problems have been spent on treatment of "alcoholics," while less than 5% has gone into prevention efforts. One reason for this distribution of resources is, as will be explained in the next section, a lack of agreement about exactly what the goals of prevention should be and what methods should be used to accomplish them.

Prevention in any form tends to be a more complicated approach to drinking problems than the approach that simply insists that alcoholics abstain from drinking. And prevention cannot help but step on the toes of some special interest groups. Everyone agrees that something should be done for those with the heaviest drinking problems, and the widespread popular appeal of the disease concept, along with its politically powerful supporters, has succeeded in making the treatment of alcoholics the focus of public policy on alcohol.

An exclusive emphasis on alcoholics and their treatment does not address the majority of drinking problems in this country. Most societal costs related to alcohol—loss of worker productivity due to absenteeism or impaired performance, automobile accidents, fires, crimes, disrupted families, health care expenses, etc.—are not caused by people who would ordinarily be labeled as alcoholics. These problems are largely ignored by public policies based on the disease concept.

With treatment programs such as Alcoholics Anonymous, individuals who want treatment must first agree that they are totally unable to deal with alcohol. In other words, they must accept the idea that they have a disease. Partly as a result of this approach, few people with drinking problems ever seek help, and even fewer from among the large numbers with the "minor" drinking problems which can be very costly to society, if not to the individual, consider treatment. They simply do not wish to view themselves as unable to handle alcohol because they are biologically or otherwise different.

Despite claims to the contrary, the failure rates for the few and generally most severe problem drinkers who do enter treatment are very high. In fact, results from studies of

a wide variety of alcoholism treatment facilities indicated that more than half of the participants have already begun drinking again within six months after discharge.

Though it is generally agreed that disease-oriented programs have helped many alcoholics, many of the problems associated with drinking are not caused by "alcoholics," and few people with any kind of drinking problem seek help. Of the severely alcohol-dependent individuals receiving treatment—often because they were forced by families, employees, or the law—only a minority experience any significant long-term improvement in their drinking status. The need for a change in public policy on alcohol seems obvious, but this also demands eradication of our society's ambivalence about drinking.

Actress Brooke Shields endorses an alcohol-education program sponsored by the National Council on Alcoholism. An independent organization supported by private donations, the council offers treatment and information about addictive drinking to people of all ages.

Models and Methods for Prevention

In recent years there has been evidence that public policies associated with alcohol have begun to focus on prevention. The National Institute on Alcohol Abuse and Alcoholism (NIAAA) has (1) promoted the stabilization of per capita alcohol consumption, (2) urged the use of warning labels to advise pregnant women of the risks of fetal alcohol syndrome, (3) supported experimentation with devices to warn or prevent drinkers from driving, and (4) criticized the advertising practices of the alcoholic beverage industry. In general, a greater focus on a public health concept of problem driving seems to be evident.

The basic goal of alcohol policy should be to prevent or reduce *any* problems associated with drinking, rather than just to find and treat alcoholics. This change is the result of the recognition of the high cost and limited effectiveness of treatment for severe drinking problems and of a general increase in the health consciousness of Americans. In addition, scientific evidence on patterns of drinking and drinking problems in the general population has played a role. It has been shown that there are not two separate groups of people, as suggested by the disease concept: one group whose alcohol consumption centers around a moderate or nonproblem drinking level, and another smaller group whose average drinking is heavy. Drinking patterns are more complicated than that, and people do not fit neatly into one category or another.

These trends and realizations have set the stage for a number of specific policy actions and proposals. Experts have described three basic categories of prevention efforts, each focusing on a particular method for reducing drinking problems: (1) *distribution* policies designed to influence drinking problems indirectly by controlling rates of per capita consumption; (2) *education and enforcement* policies, which attempt to shape acceptable drinking practices mainly by calling attention to inappropriate or unsafe practices; and (3) *environmental safety* policies, which seek to make the world safer for alcohol-impaired persons and those around them. Some examples of these approaches are discussed below.

Distribution

Distribution approaches to prevention are based on two assumptions. One is that if alcoholic beverages are made more difficult to obtain, less alcohol will be consumed. The second is that cutting the overall, or per capita, rate of consumption will result in a reduction of alcohol-related problems. Evidence for these assumptions is available from the United States' experience with Prohibition, as well as from outcomes associated with several other historical events and policies.

Contrary to popular belief, the goal of Prohibition—to reduce drinking and its problems—was met, and probably would have been achieved with even greater success had the government been more determined to enforce the policy. During the period from 1919 to 1933 the rates of both general alcohol consumption *and* alcoholism (as measured by deaths due to cirrhosis of the liver) decreased significantly. Similar effects were observed in areas of Europe where wines and other alcoholic beverages were rationed or in short supply during World War II. Finland experienced a significant drop in public drunkenness and alcohol-related visits to hospitals and clinics when lengthy strikes by liquor store workers decreased alcohol availability.

Cross-cultural and domestic comparisons also suggest that the higher the cost of alcoholic beverages, particularly when taxes are used to increase cost, the lower the rate of per capita consumption and deaths due to alcohol-related medical problems. One recent study of liquor taxes in 30 states revealed that increases of as little as 1% to 10% could reduce alcohol consumption, highway fatalities, and deaths due to cirrhosis. Thus, drinking problems appear to be sensitive to the cost of alcohol.

It may even be that increases in Americans' consumption of alcohol since 1960 are partly due to the fact that the cost of alcohol has not nearly kept pace with inflation. Thus, we may be drinking more because it is relatively cheaper to do so than it was some years ago. Also, since 1960 the kinds and numbers of outlets selling and/or serving alcohol have expanded dramatically, as have the hours of operation for such distributors. This increased availability may also contribute to greater alcohol use.

One final distribution method for preventing drinking problems is minimum drinking age laws. Legal drinking ages have varied considerably over the past 20 years, first decreasing in many states during the Vietnam War era, and then, more recently, increasing. It seems likely that within a few years federal government policies will force all states to set the age at 21.

Much of the pressure to raise drinking ages came from concern that the earlier lowerings had increased alcohol consumption by young people and led to significantly increased risks of drinking problems, most notably involvement in alcohol-related automobile accidents. In fact, there is good evidence to indicate that lower drinking ages were

how do you say "no" to a drink?

Saying no to a drink isn't always easy. Sometimes it's extremely difficult and requires a lot of thought, practice, and support. We want to help by offering some practical suggestions which we hope you'll find helpful. You may want to try a few out to see which ones work best for you, and to see which ones you are most comfortable using...

* No, thanks, I want to stay in control.

* No, thanks, I want to be in the driver's seat.

* No, thanks, I don't want to get into trouble with my parents (teachers, friends, grandparents, and so forth).

* No, thanks, if I drink I'll lose my privileges (e.g., use of the car).

* No thanks, I don't like the taste.

* No thanks, I don't drink.

* No thanks, it's just not me.

* No, thanks, I've got to study later (or pick up a friend, or get up early, and so forth).

* No, thanks, I want to keep a clear head.

* No, thanks, I usually end up embarrassing myself.

* No, thanks, "real teens" don't need to drink.

* No, thanks, drinking makes me tired.

* No, thanks, I don't want to gain any weight.

* No, thanks, I'm in training.

* No, thanks, what else have you got?

* No, thanks.

You may want to develop your own refusal skills, and more importantly, you may wish to get support from your friends, parents, and teachers for saying no. Being able to say no often takes courage and certainly shows that you value yourself, your relationship with your family, and, that you are handling things in an adult manner. Asking for help is also a very mature thing to do.

HOW DO YOU SAY NO TO A DRINK?

ANY WAY YOU WANT TO!!!

****
Brought to you by...

National Institute on
Alcohol Abuse and Alcoholism

PREVENTION PIPELINE

associated with such changes, though the size of these increases has probably been exaggerated. In addition, the extent to which these alcohol-related problems were due only and directly to lower drinking ages is unclear.

Data which pertain to the question of whether or not raising legal drinking ages will successfully reverse these effects are limited at this time. However, most experts agree that some positive impact in terms of reduced drinking and drinking problems in the affected (and younger) age groups can be expected.

Despite the apparent effectiveness of prevention through control of availability or access to alcohol, the method has had difficulty gaining acceptance. This is not so much because it fails at its stated purpose, but because people resist it in principle, feeling that this method costs special interest groups money and is liable to have negative side effects. Governmental restriction of alcohol use is seen by many as a constraint on individual liberty, which has no place in a free and democratic society in which public policies should reflect the wishes of the people (in this case as indicated by current drinking practices). Yet, another purpose of government is to preserve the welfare of its people, and if this goal

A modern "moonshiner" tests the output of his backwoods still near Ukiah, California. Such illicit activity was widespread during Prohibition, but is relatively rare today.

can be furthered by a limited constraint (of alcohol use), then, arguably, it should be pursued.

Such conflicts are not easily resolved in a society that is ambivalent about drinking, especially when the alcoholic beverage industry and those with a vested interest in disease-oriented alcoholism treatment can be viewed as resistant to broad-spectrum prevention efforts, such as those involving distribution control. One result has been that, with rare exceptions such as the outlawing of "happy hours" in Massachusetts, recent distribution measures have been directed mainly at those with limited political power, young people in particular. The inconsistency of present policy is further evidenced by the continued expansion of general availability of alcohol, while restrictions on youthful use are being tightened.

The fact that many minors drink anyway provides an illustration of how distribution policies can have negative side effects and how merely raising the legal drinking age fails. Young people know they are not the only ones with alcohol problems, or even the ones with the worst problems, so understandably they resent the double standard which works against them. The backlash of anger may be expressed in more than just a specific disregard of the minimum drinking age. It may carry over to create a more general disrespect for the law, which seriously undermines society.

Making alcohol an illegal drug for more young people may encourage their use of other, perhaps more dangerous, illicit drugs, since the distinctions between society's view of different drug types would be minimized. Indeed, some experts have argued that the apparently declining adolescent use of illicit drugs in recent years can be traced to the legalization and growing availability of alcohol for teenagers. Thus, the changing of drinking patterns in this group may simply result in the substitution of one drug problem for another.

The potential for negative side effects from distribution restrictions is not limited to young people, as the experience of Prohibition has shown. Despite some positive outcomes in diminishing specific alcohol problems, that extreme effort to stop alcohol distribution altogether stimulated moonshining and bootlegging, growth of the criminal underworld,

121

and corruption of government officials. Such extensive violations of the law and other negative consequences of Prohibition eventually led the public to decide that the social price of reducing drinking problems by this method was too high.

As a result, there now seems to be a prejudice against any general alcohol control as a means of prevention. Opponents argue that it would return us to the nightmare of Prohibition. In all probability, marked increases in taxes on alcohol and/or excessive restriction of outlets or outlet hours would lead to a certain amount of illegal production and sales. Nevertheless, limited use of distribution measures has a place in a comprehensive program for preventing drinking problems.

Education and Enforcement

Many prevention efforts focus on education. Along with the formulation and enforcement of alcohol-related laws and regulations, it represents a *sociocultural* approach to prevention. In other words, the ultimate goal is to shape social and cultural norms about drinking in such a way that typical patterns of alcohol consumption produce a minimum of drinking problems.

Developing programs to accomplish such a goal is extremely difficult in this society because the wide variety and often conflicting content of messages about drinking result in considerable ambiguity about the appropriate use of alcohol. Thus, if implemented without the support of other programs and broad changes in the media and in people's attitudes, the common educational method of increasing knowledge and hoping for positive attitude and behavior

Students Against Driving Drunk

SADD (Students Against Driving Drunk) is a national organization whose student-led, high-school-based chapters work to offset peer pressure to drink or to drive while under the influence of alcohol. SADD encourages teenagers to call their parents for transportation rather than drive with anyone who has been drinking.

change is liable to produce more ambivalence about drinking rather than more well-thought-out decisions about alcohol use.

The general ineffectiveness of simple presentations of factual messages, especially exaggerated or one-sided "scare" tactics, has been amply demonstrated in the repeated failures of public information media campaigns related to drinking problems. Perhaps focusing on more accurate and less glamorous presentations of alcohol and its effects in media advertising and programming would have more impact. It seems unrealistic to have expected that a few public service announcements could compete with hours of well-produced ads and shows promoting drinking in both obvious and subtle ways.

The results of school- and community-based alcohol education efforts have been similar. To be effective in changing current or future drinking behavior these programs must do more than just present facts. They must involve an opportunity to blend information with the existing and developing values and behavioral skills of each individual. Consequently, the most promising programs are those that encourage personal involvement in: (1) open discussions with peers and self-awareness exercises that help participants clarify their values and goals with respect to drinking, and (2) instruction and role-playing of assertive skills that build self-confidence and promote better management of

In 1939 federal agents found this cache of illegal alcohol behind a secret sliding door in a Kansas City basement. The repeal of Prohibition laws put most U.S. bootleggers out of business, but a few still continue to defy the law by selling untaxed liquor.

real-life situations involving alcohol. When teenagers are involved, the inclusion of parents can also be important.

Both in school and at home, instruction and modeling should provide a consistent message that in any environment there is never any reason for drinking to be expected or needed. In situations in which drinking may occur, everyone should be taught how to use alcohol responsibly.

Some simple facts can be very helpful to successful efforts at moderation. For example, understanding how number of drinks, rate of drinking, and body weight determine BAC (and the effects of alcohol) is essential to setting appropriate limits. Knowing to eat before and during drinking, to use weak alcoholic beverages, to drink slowly, and to space the drinks is also useful. The main point of alcohol education, however, should always be to focus on questions related to expectations—how does drinking help you achieve your goals, and what alternative ways exist which would

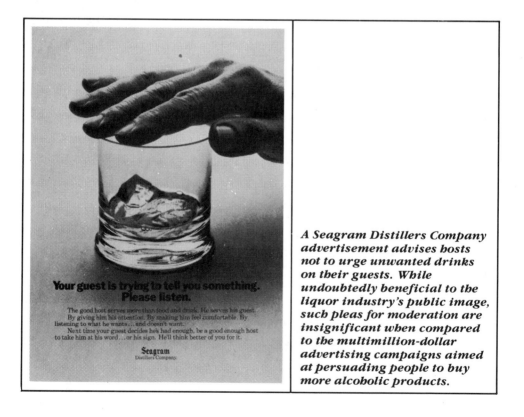

Your guest is trying to tell you something.
Please listen.

The good host serves more than food and drink. He serves his guest.
By giving him his attention. By making him feel comfortable. By listening to what he wants... and doesn't want.
Next time your guest decides he's had enough, be a good enough host to take him at his word... or his sign. He'll think better of you for it.

Seagram
Distillers Company.

A Seagram Distillers Company advertisement advises hosts not to urge unwanted drinks on their guests. While undoubtedly beneficial to the liquor industry's public image, such pleas for moderation are insignificant when compared to the multimillion-dollar advertising campaigns aimed at persuading people to buy more alcoholic products.

accomplish these goals as well or better, without alcohol's risks?

Law enforcement is another form of sociocultural prevention that may discourage unsafe or inappropriate drinking practices. Probably the best example is the recent attention given to stricter enforcement of drunk driving laws and efforts to increase the harshness and certainty of punishment of those convicted of such offenses.

Results of early studies on these measures gave reason

for optimism. Dramatic decreases in alcohol-related accidents and fatalities were reported in a number of jurisdic-
tions after tougher drunk-driving laws were enacted. Unfortunately, these effects generally proved to be short-lived.
Apparently people came to realize that, although potential
penalties were more severe, the chances of getting caught
were still extremely slim. (It is estimated that only about
one in 2000 drunk drivers will ever be arrested). Moreover,
because of an overloaded court system, overcrowded jails,
and numerous legal technicalities, punishment often was not
swift, severe, or even certain. As a result the statistics on
alcohol-related incidents crept back up.

Actually, these results should have been expected given
what is known about the effectiveness of punishment in

*A Michigan state
trooper detains a
suspected drunken
driver in 1947. The
breath-testing device is
an "intoximeter," a
rather primitive-
looking tool used as an
aid in enforcing
drunk-driving laws.*

controlling behavior. It has been shown that, in general, for punishment to be most effective it should be delivered quickly and consistently each time the problem behavior is performed. Thus, the severity of the punishment is not a strong factor if it rarely follows the behavior. Why then should the remote threat of a possible jail sentence or substantial fine be expected to have much of an effect?

Alternatively, there is some evidence to suggest that beefing up enforcement efforts to increase the certainty of being caught if driving drunk would have a much greater impact than making penalties harsher. Unfortunately, a significant change in law enforcement along this line is extremely expensive. Given this consideration, society has shown a preference for symbolic and piecemeal approaches, such as increasing penalties or increasing the drinking age. These kinds of interventions meet little resistance and perhaps better reflect our ambivalence about drinking and our reluctance to confront its associated problems directly.

Ironically, one legal change regarding drinking may even have increased our problems with it. The decriminalization of public drunkenness, based on the disease concept notion that the alcoholic is not responsible for his or her behavior and needs treatment rather than punishment, could lead to greater use of drinking as an excuse or explanation for undesirable behavior. In fact, there is some evidence to suggest that growing numbers of people in alcoholism treatment are there because the courts seem to go easier on those who claim their offenses were caused by alcohol and so they should get help rather than be penalized.

Effective use of any law to change drinking habits and reduce drinking problems is very complicated and difficult, exaggerated by the need to foresee negative side effects.

Environmental Safety

Lastly, prevention policies can focus on the reduction of environmental risks for drinkers and those around them. This approach does not prevent alcohol use and abuse directly, but dampens the consequences of drinking. Encouraging or requiring use of passive restraints or other automobile safety devices might be one easy way to minimize drunk-driving problems both for the drunk and anyone else on the road. Although the number of alcohol-related accidents might remain the same, there would be fewer deaths and serious injuries. It might also be worthwhile to permit or insist that those around an intoxicated person take steps to ensure his or her safety. This might involve, for example, refusing further alcohol service to a drunken guest or patron, or providing transportation for such individuals.

These physical or social safety measures may strike you as intruding too much on your individual choices and rights and/or those of the drinker. Safer cars will cost more; and why should someone else decide when a person has had too much to drink and then feel obligated to do something about it? You may also feel that drinkers should be made to pay for their mistakes, and others should not have to be responsible for them. Each of these objections may have some merit, though it is worth remembering that the mistake could be made by you or someone you care about, or could directly or indirectly affect you. And these kinds of measures would undoubtedly help preserve the general well-being of our citizens by reducing the negative consequences of excessive drinking. In that sense, they are truly prevention measures in the interest of public health and as such are certainly worth considering.

Conclusion

An examination of American public policy on problem drinking reveals that it is still another area where our ambivalence about alcohol is evident. There is no clear and

In 1979 The Museum of the City of New York exhibited this assemblage to illustrate dramatically the agonies and consequences of alcohol abuse.

single-minded plan to deal with the drinking issue. Instead, policymakers have accepted the simplistic disease concept of alcoholism, ignoring scientific evidence and well-reasoned recommendations while taking only those actions that are not objectionable to large and politically powerful interests. The result has been a heavy investment of resources in just one area (treatment) for only one group (alcoholics) that represents but a small part of the drinking problems of this country. And, the results for even this small group have been largely unsuccessful.

The time has come to review our public health priorities and to explore some alternative approaches to problem drinking. Prevention efforts, involving a carefully considered combination of distribution control, education/enforcement efforts, and environmental safety measures would appear to be one promising alternative to present policy. There is some indication that a growing health consciousness in the American public could help make this possible.

Coming to grips with our ambivalence about the social meaning of drinking is essential. Though this is clearly not just a problem for teenagers, they may represent one of the best groups with which to start. After all, they will shape alcohol policy for the next generation to come.

APPENDIX

STATE AGENCIES
FOR THE PREVENTION AND TREATMENT
OF DRUG ABUSE

ALABAMA

Department of Mental Health
Division of Mental Illness and
    Substance Abuse Community
    Programs
200 Interstate Park Drive
P.O. Box 3710
Montgomery, AL 36193
(205) 271-9253

ALASKA

Department of Health and Social
    Services
Office of Alcoholism and Drug
    Abuse
Pouch H-05-F
Juneau, AK 99811
(907) 586-6201

ARIZONA

Department of Health Services
Division of Behavioral Health
    Services
Bureau of Community Services
Alcohol Abuse and Alcoholism
    Section
2500 East Van Buren
Phoenix, AZ 85008
(602) 255-1238

Department of Health Services
Division of Behavioral Health
    Services
Bureau of Community Services
Drug Abuse Section
2500 East Van Buren
Phoenix, AZ 85008
(602) 255-1240

ARKANSAS

Department of Human Services
Office on Alcohol and Drug Abuse
    Prevention
1515 West 7th Avenue
Suite 310
Little Rock, AR 72202
(501) 371-2603

CALIFORNIA

Department of Alcohol and Drug
    Abuse
111 Capitol Mall
Sacramento, CA 95814
(916) 445-1940

COLORADO

Department of Health
Alcohol and Drug Abuse Division
4210 East 11th Avenue
Denver, CO 80220
(303) 320-6137

CONNECTICUT

Alcohol and Drug Abuse
    Commission
999 Asylum Avenue
3rd Floor
Hartford, CT 06105
(203) 566-4145

DELAWARE

Division of Mental Health
Bureau of Alcoholism and Drug
    Abuse
1901 North Dupont Highway
Newcastle, DE 19720
(302) 421-6101

DISTRICT OF COLUMBIA
Department of Human Services
Office of Health Planning and
 Development
601 Indiana Avenue, NW
Suite 500
Washington, D.C. 20004
(202) 724-5641

FLORIDA
Department of Health and
 Rehabilitative Services
Alcoholic Rehabilitation Program
1317 Winewood Boulevard
Room 187A
Tallahassee, FL 32301
(904) 488-0396

Department of Health and
 Rehabilitative Services
Drug Abuse Program
1317 Winewood Boulevard
Building 6, Room 155
Tallahassee, FL 32301
(904) 488-0900

GEORGIA
Department of Human Resources
Division of Mental Health and
 Mental Retardation
Alcohol and Drug Section
618 Ponce De Leon Avenue, NE
Atlanta, GA 30365-2101
(404) 894-4785

HAWAII
Department of Health
Mental Health Division
Alcohol and Drug Abuse Branch
1250 Punch Bowl Street
P.O. Box 3378
Honolulu, HI 96801
(808) 548-4280

IDAHO
Department of Health and Welfare
Bureau of Preventive Medicine
Substance Abuse Section
450 West State
Boise, ID 83720
(208) 334-4368

ILLINOIS
Department of Mental Health and
 Developmental Disabilities
Division of Alcoholism
160 North La Salle Street
Room 1500
Chicago, IL 60601
(312) 793-2907

Illinois Dangerous Drugs
 Commission
300 North State Street
Suite 1500
Chicago, IL 60610
(312) 822-9860

INDIANA
Department of Mental Health
Division of Addiction Services
429 North Pennsylvania Street
Indianapolis, IN 46204
(317) 232-7816

IOWA
Department of Substance Abuse
505 5th Avenue
Insurance Exchange Building
Suite 202
Des Moines, IA 50319
(515) 281-3641

KANSAS
Department of Social Rehabilitation
Alcohol and Drug Abuse Services
2700 West 6th Street
Biddle Building
Topeka, KS 66606
(913) 296-3925

KENTUCKY
Cabinet for Human Resources
Department of Health Services
Substance Abuse Branch
275 East Main Street
Frankfort, KY 40601
(502) 564-2880

LOUISIANA
Department of Health and Human
 Resources
Office of Mental Health and
 Substance Abuse
655 North 5th Street
P.O. Box 4049
Baton Rouge, LA 70821
(504) 342-2565

MAINE
Department of Human Services
Office of Alcoholism and Drug
 Abuse Prevention
Bureau of Rehabilitation
32 Winthrop Street
Augusta, ME 04330
(207) 289-2781

MARYLAND
Alcoholism Control Administration
201 West Preston Street
Fourth Floor
Baltimore, MD 21201
(301) 383-2977

State Health Department
Drug Abuse Administration
201 West Preston Street
Baltimore, MD 21201
(301) 383-3312

MASSACHUSETTS
Department of Public Health
Division of Alcoholism
755 Boylston Street
Sixth Floor
Boston, MA 02116
(617) 727-1960

Department of Public Health
Division of Drug Rehabilitation
600 Washington Street
Boston, MA 02114
(617) 727-8617

MICHIGAN
Department of Public Health
Office of Substance Abuse Services
3500 North Logan Street
P.O. Box 30035
Lansing, MI 48909
(517) 373-8603

MINNESOTA
Department of Public Welfare
Chemical Dependency Program
 Division
Centennial Building
658 Cedar Street
4th Floor
Saint Paul, MN 55155
(612) 296-4614

MISSISSIPPI
Department of Mental Health
Division of Alcohol and Drug Abuse
1102 Robert E. Lee Building
Jackson, MS 39201
(601) 359-1297

MISSOURI
Department of Mental Health
Division of Alcoholism and Drug
 Abuse
2002 Missouri Boulevard
P.O. Box 687
Jefferson City, MO 65102
(314) 751-4942

MONTANA
Department of Institutions
Alcohol and Drug Abuse Division
1539 11th Avenue
Helena, MT 59620
(406) 449-2827

NEBRASKA
Department of Public Institutions
Division of Alcoholism and Drug Abuse
801 West Van Dorn Street
P.O. Box 94728
Lincoln, NB 68509
(402) 471-2851, Ext. 415

NEVADA
Department of Human Resources
Bureau of Alcohol and Drug Abuse
505 East King Street
Carson City, NV 89710
(702) 885-4790

NEW HAMPSHIRE
Department of Health and Welfare
Office of Alcohol and Drug Abuse
  Prevention
Hazen Drive
Health and Welfare Building
Concord, NH 03301
(603) 271-4627

NEW JERSEY
Department of Health
Division of Alcoholism
129 East Hanover Street CN 362
Trenton, NJ 08625
(609) 292-8949

Department of Health
Division of Narcotic and Drug Abuse
  Control
129 East Hanover Street CN 362
Trenton, NJ 08625
(609) 292-8949

NEW MEXICO
Health and Environment Department
Behavioral Services Division
Substance Abuse Bureau
725 Saint Michaels Drive
P.O. Box 968
Santa Fe, NM 87503
(505) 984-0020, Ext. 304

NEW YORK
Division of Alcoholism and Alcohol
  Abuse
194 Washington Avenue
Albany, NY 12210
(518) 474-5417

Division of Substance Abuse
  Services
Executive Park South
Box 8200
Albany, NY 12203
(518) 457-7629

NORTH CAROLINA
Department of Human Resources
Division of Mental Health, Mental
  Retardation and Substance Abuse
  Services
Alcohol and Drug Abuse Services
325 North Salisbury Street
Albemarle Building
Raleigh, NC 27611
(919) 733-4670

NORTH DAKOTA
Department of Human Services
Division of Alcoholism and Drug
  Abuse
State Capitol Building
Bismarck, ND 58505
(701) 224-2767

OHIO
Department of Health
Division of Alcoholism
246 North High Street
P.O. Box 118
Columbus, OH 43216
(614) 466-3543

Department of Mental Health
Bureau of Drug Abuse
65 South Front Street
Columbus, OH 43215
(614) 466-9023

OKLAHOMA
Department of Mental Health
Alcohol and Drug Programs
4545 North Lincoln Boulevard
Suite 100 East Terrace
P.O. Box 53277
Oklahoma City, OK 73152
(405) 521-0044

OREGON
Department of Human Resources
Mental Health Division
Office of Programs for Alcohol and
  Drug Problems
2575 Bittern Street, NE
Salem, OR 97310
(503) 378-2163

PENNSYLVANIA
Department of Health
Office of Drug and Alcohol
  Programs
Commonwealth and Forster Avenues
Health and Welfare Building
P.O. Box 90
Harrisburg, PA 17108
(717) 787-9857

RHODE ISLAND
Department of Mental Health,
  Mental Retardation and Hospitals
Division of Substance Abuse
Substance Abuse Administration
  Building
Cranston, RI 02920
(401) 464-2091

SOUTH CAROLINA
Commission on Alcohol and Drug
  Abuse
3700 Forest Drive
Columbia, SC 29204
(803) 758-2521

SOUTH DAKOTA
Department of Health
Division of Alcohol and Drug Abuse
523 East Capitol, Joe Foss Building
Pierre, SD 57501
(605) 773-4806

TENNESSEE
Department of Mental Health and
  Mental Retardation
Alcohol and Drug Abuse Services
505 Deaderick Street
James K. Polk Building, Fourth Floor
Nashville, TN 37219
(615) 741-1921

TEXAS
Commission on Alcoholism
809 Sam Houston State Office Building
Austin, TX 78701
(512) 475-2577

Department of Community Affairs
Drug Abuse Prevention Division
2015 South Interstate Highway 35
P.O. Box 13166
Austin, TX 78711
(512) 443-4100

UTAH
Department of Social Services
Division of Alcoholism and Drugs
150 West North Temple
Suite 350
P.O. Box 2500
Salt Lake City, UT 84110
(801) 533-6532

VERMONT
Agency of Human Services
Department of Social and
  Rehabilitation Services
Alcohol and Drug Abuse Division
103 South Main Street
Waterbury, VT 05676
(802) 241-2170

VIRGINIA

Department of Mental Health and
Mental Retardation
Division of Substance Abuse
109 Governor Street
P.O. Box 1797
Richmond, VA 23214
(804) 786-5313

WASHINGTON

Department of Social and Health
Service
Bureau of Alcohol and Substance
Abuse
Office Building—44 W
Olympia, WA 98504
(206) 753-5866

WEST VIRGINIA

Department of Health
Office of Behavioral Health Services
Division on Alcoholism and Drug
Abuse
1800 Washington Street East
Building 3 Room 451
Charleston, WV 25305
(304) 348-2276

WISCONSIN

Department of Health and Social
Services
Division of Community Services
Bureau of Community Programs
Alcohol and Other Drug Abuse
Program Office
1 West Wilson Street
P.O. Box 7851
Madison, WI 53707
(608) 266-2717

WYOMING

Alcohol and Drug Abuse Programs
Hathaway Building
Cheyenne, WY 82002
(307) 777-7115, Ext. 7118

GUAM

Mental Health & Substance Abuse
Agency
P.O. Box 20999
Guam 96921

PUERTO RICO

Department of Addiction Control
Services
Alcohol Abuse Programs
P.O. Box B-Y Rio Piedras Station
Rio Piedras, PR 00928
(809) 763-5014

Department of Addiction Control
Services
Drug Abuse Programs
P.O. Box B-Y Rio Piedras Station
Rio Piedras, PR 00928
(809) 764-8140

VIRGIN ISLANDS

Division of Mental Health,
Alcoholism & Drug Dependency
Services
P.O. Box 7329
Saint Thomas, Virgin Islands 00801
(809) 774-7265

AMERICAN SAMOA

LBJ Tropical Medical Center
Department of Mental Health Clinic
Pago Pago, American Samoa 96799

TRUST TERRITORIES

Director of Health Services
Office of the High Commissioner
Saipan, Trust Territories 96950

Further Reading

Claypool, Jane. *Alcohol and Teens.* New York: Messner, 1984.

——————. *Alcohol and You.* New York: Franklin Watts, 1981.

Cross, Wilbur. *Kids and Booze: What You Must Know to Help Them.* New York: E P Dutton, 1979.

Englehardt, Stanley L. *Kids and Alcohol, the Deadliest Drug.* New York: Lothrop, 1975.

Greene, Shep. *The Boy Who Drank Too Much.* New York: Viking, 1979.

Howard, Marion. *Did I Have a Good Time?* New York: Continuum, 1982.

Langone, John. *Bombed, Buzzed, Smashed...or Sober.* New York: Avon, 1979.

Milgram, Gail G. *Coping with Alcohol.* New York: Rosen Group, 1980.

North, Robert J. and Orange, Richard A., jr. *Teenage Drinking: The Number One Drug Problem in America Today.* New York: Macmillan, 1980.

Reiners, Kenneth G. *There's More to Life than Pumpkins, Drugs & Other False Gods.* Wayzata, Minnesota: Woodland, 1980.

Young, Lawrence, et al. *America's Number One Teenage Drug Problem.* Seattle: Vulcan Books, 1981.

Index

Alan R. Lang, Ph.D., received his degree from the University of Wisconsin and is currently an associate professor of psychology at Florida State University. He has written many articles for scientific journals including a widely cited report on personality factors and addictive behavior which he prepared for the National Academy of Sciences.

Solomon H. Snyder, M.D., is Distinguished Service Professor of Neuroscience, Pharmacology and Psychiatry at The Johns Hopkins University School of Medicine. He has served as president of the Society for Neuroscience and in 1978 received the Albert Lasker Award in Medical Research. He has authored *Uses of Marijuana, Madness and the Brain, The Troubled Mind, Biological Aspects of Mental Disorder,* and edited *Perspective in Neuropharmacology: A Tribute to Julius Axelrod.* Professor Snyder was a research associate with Dr. Axelrod at the National Institutes of Health.

Barry L. Jacobs, Ph.D., is currently a professor in the program of neuroscience at Princeton University. Professor Jacobs is author of *Serotonin Neurotransmission and Behavior* and *Hallucinogens: Neuro-chemical, Behavioral and Clinical Perspectives.* He has written many journal articles in the field of neuroscience and contributed numerous chapters to books on behavior and brain science. He has been a member of several panels of the National Institute of Mental Health.

Jerome H. Jaffe, M.D., formerly professor of psychiatry at the College of Physicians and Surgeons, Columbia University, has been named recently Director of the Addiction Research Center of the National Institute on Drug Abuse. Dr. Jaffe is also a psychopharmacologist and has conducted research on a wide range of addictive drugs and developed treatment programs for addicts. He has acted as Special Consultant to the President on Narcotics and Dangerous Drugs and was the first director of the White House Special Action Office for Drug Abuse Prevention.